The
Insatiable Gardener's
Guide

How to Grow Anything &
Everything Indoors,
Year 'Round

By Susan M. Brackney

published by Five Hearts Press

Five Hearts Press
7854 North State Road 37
Bloomington, Indiana 47404

Publisher's Cataloging-In-Publication Data

Brackney, Susan M.
The insatiable gardener's guide: how to grow anything & everything indoors,
year 'round / by Susan M. Brackney. -- 1st American ed.
p. : ill. ; cm.
Includes index.
ISBN: 0-9746788-0-5
1. Indoor gardening. 2. House plants. I. Title.

SB419 .B73 2004
635.9/65   2003097789

Published in the United States
2004
1st American edition

Cover design by Ty Connally
Illustrations by Susan M. Brackney
Layout and typesetting by Patrick Petro

Typeset in 11 point Minion (Slimbach, 1989)

for Charles C. Deam

Contents

The Insatiable Parts

Chapter 1

Carrots & the Great Outdoors

It was surely the carrots that started all this. First, their feathery crowns the color of fresh limes. Then a hint of pale root and, not long after, row upon row of the orange root tops swelling out of the ground. I was just six when I had my first garden. It was a sandy patch planted full of carrots and nothing else because, I reasoned, no other vegetables were any good anyway.

It didn't take long for me to realize I was hooked on the sweet expectation that only a garden can bring. In the case of the carrots, for instance, I watched them go from hard seeds to tall greens, and to the best part—the orange surprise.

Even now I'm still in awe of the natural cycles of the garden. Whether I'm growing cayenne peppers, tomatoes, or eggplants, I am always caught a little off guard when I notice the first fruits. *It worked!*

I feel like crying. It's not just relief that I succeeded at something. Rather, it's knowing that keeping up hope and working hard still pay off. It's comforting to know that even though the world is filled with so much discord and uncertainty, my garden is a sure bet—well, most of the time anyway. Sometimes raccoons ravage my sweet corn and the birds get all the berries. Nevertheless, a garden is a hopeful thing, and we all need something to look forward to.

the Haves & Me

For years, I was something of a nomad, moving from one soulless apartment to another while working my way through college. I was hungry for a garden of my own but I had no land. At one point I had access to a four-by-five-foot patio, and I tried growing vegetables and flowers in a raised bed there. My friend built me a bottomless box that I then filled with heavy topsoil. Of course, with such

inadequate drainage and soil depth, my plants died and I was left with an ugly box of mud. In the coming years I had more success with balcony gardens full of potted tomatoes and zinnias, but it still wasn't quite enough.

I found a way to get my gardening fix at least temporarily by offering to work other people's land for them. Between my many horticulturally challenged friends, I picked a new spot to garden every year so no one would feel left out. I performed nutrient assays, amended the soil as needed, and grew enough food for each of us to share.

I'll never forget the time I handed over the first sugar-snap pea of the season to a friend who had never before tasted one. I showed him how to peel away the string and watched as he put the whole pod in his mouth. Chewing slowly. Smiling now. Amazed, he asked, "Did you water these with a sugar solution?"

But having to drive out to my garden every day or so to cultivate, water, and monitor the overall progress got old. Not to mention the fact that I was always starting over each year. That meant I wasn't able to make important adjustments based on past success in a particular area. Worst of all was knowing I had a lush garden going and I couldn't just wander through it at all hours of the day or night without making a spectacle of myself.

See, if I could, I would stay out in the garden for hours just sitting, meditating, trying to perceive growth in real time. I would wait patiently as buds gave way to petals and petals gave way to seeds. I would wait and wait and wait as the tomatoes turned and green beans presented themselves one by one. Eventually, though, my back would start to ache and the mosquitoes would extract most of my blood. And, before you know it, bill collectors are looking for me, my hair has grown down to my ankles, and, inexplicably, I am covered in snow.

The La-ti-da Greenhouses

I thought maybe indoor growing might be a practical solution to my insatiability, and I had my first taste of indoor gardening when I worked on a wealthy woman's estate as her Master Gardener's assistant. She was an important philanthropist, and her gardens, mansion, greenhouses, and the resident Master Gardener's cottage occupied an entire city block.

Built in 1910, the outdoor gardens were designed after a garden in Pompeii. The benefactress made sure they were open to the public

5

during much of the year and I worked in them occasionally, keeping the place tidy and taking cuttings of some of the more unusual herb strains.

I got to spend most of my time, however, in her amazing greenhouse. It was a traditional glass house with many rooms, and there were concrete floors equipped with drains throughout. All hoses and tools were to be carefully maintained per the lady's exacting specifications, and all trash and plant debris had to be collected and neatly disposed of at once.

As he showed me where to keep the hoses, the gardener told me this: "The hose has a memory. It remembers how it likes to be wound up. Respect its preference and your hose will last and last."

The orchids had their own area, as did the indoor cut-flower gardens. In particular, she must've had an affinity for carnations because she had tables and tables full of them. They grew up through a carefully stringed grid to keep every flower nice and straight.

6

Unfortunately, she also preferred chemical pesticides, herbicides, and artificial rooting hormones, and their odors permeated the greenhouse along with the exotic floral notes. I wished her greenhouse were mine. I made a long list of things I would do differently if it were.

It didn't take me long to fully grasp that I was wishing well beyond my means. Part of the Master Gardener's job description included making sure she always had fresh cut flowers throughout her mansion, and part of my job description was following the Master Gardener around inside with a diminutive broom and dustpan. I swept up dead leaves and old flower heads before they even hit the floor. I kept quiet and kept my head down for the most part. But there was one day when I sneaked a glance around. I saw an original Picasso on one wall and a remarkable marble-topped table. Its center had been cut out to accommodate a natural pool on top of which floated live lily pads. Did I mention the original Henry Moore sculpture in her private yard? I began to think greenhouses were only meant for the very rich.

Until I began working at my second greenhouse, that is. This one was constructed of piping and heavy plastic. Gravel covered the ground and any stray seeds or thinned seedlings that landed there invariably took root and grew up through the gravel with no trouble. (Certainly, the philanthropist wouldn't have approved.) This was a much smaller, commercial operation—an organic farm— where no artificial pesticides, herbicides, or chemical fertilizers of any kind were used. In addition to working out in the fields harvesting and bundling herbs and flowers for the Saturday market, I blended potting medium, started seeds, and transplanted seedlings in the greenhouse, which, although much smaller than my first, always smelled wonderfully earthy in comparison.

Funny, but I never actually met the benefactress in person. By contrast, I frequently worked alongside the husband-and-wife owners of the organic farm.

Some of the seedlings we started in the greenhouse were so tiny we could hardly see them, and the husband took to using a jeweler's loupe. He would wear it all screwed up in his eye like a monocle. And if he wasn't wearing his pith helmet—complete with solar-powered fan—then odds were good that he had his yellow, radio headset tuned to Rush Limbaugh whom he despised. His loud, one-sided arguments with Rush rang out all over the farm!

I gained so much invaluable organic gardening experience from those farmers, but, more importantly I was steeped in a can-do atmosphere, which would help me to plant the seeds of things to come.

The farmers weren't exactly made of money, but they were able to have a greenhouse and they could garden year 'round if they chose. Still, even if I did have enough money to build myself a greenhouse, I had no land on which to put it.

8

Aha!

And then a light came on. Literally. It had started innocently enough with fluorescent tubes. I began starting seeds indoors under my futon to get a jump on the spring. Well before the temperature and soil outside had warmed, I had zinnias, basil, tomatoes, and catnip flourishing there. Situating myself for optimal plant viewing was no trouble; I'd lie on my stomach and hang my head over the side of my futon to glimpse the green beauties.

The pastime helped make early spring much more bearable for me, but, whether it was greed or arrogance or, I prefer to think, just an overwhelming bout of insatiability, things spiraled out of control. I was forever pushing the envelope of reasonability, and each year I would plant my seeds just a bit earlier than the year before. Late March had always been a fine time to start seeds, but I wondered if late February might not be even better. Or Valentine's Day. Or . . . New Year's Day!

I had finally pressed my luck. It had started out well at first, but then the Early Girl tomatoes and all the rest could no longer get all that they needed under that futon. Their stems grew so long and spindly that they fell over in a yellowing heap. However, as with an especially ugly baby, visitors peering in at my seedlings felt obliged to congratulate me.

In an unusual turn of events, I wished I could slow their growth. Turns out I couldn't even save them. Sure, I had plenty of time to replant, but I felt the kind of guilt only a truly insatiable gardener knows. I assured all the remaining seeds in their packages that they would never see the same fate. Of course, I wasn't sure how I would be able to control myself and keep that promise.

I did my best to resist temptation the following year, but it wasn't long before I found myself facing the shameful predicament again. I mentioned my troubles to a friend and he showed me the light.

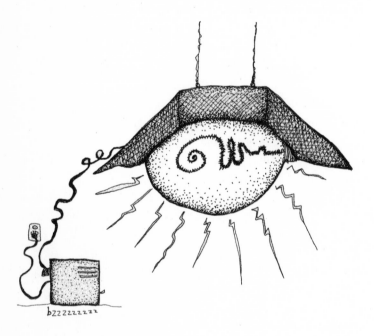

bzzzzzzzzz

In fact, he let me borrow it for a while. He had been growing all sorts of herbs and vegetables in his home for years with a special kind of lamp that I never even knew existed. It was a 1000-watt metal halide lamp, and it was like having a little piece of the sun in my garage.

Everything grew terrifically well. My zinnias even had buds by the time it was safe to put them outside. Now I was really hooked. I have since discovered a network of indoor growers who don't even bother with the outdoors! I have seen their voluptuous Swiss chard and innumerable banana peppers grown to maturity in the middle of winter.

Just as summer gardening had always been an important source of hope to me, I now know that I can keep that hope alive during the grayest winter days—even without a fancy greenhouse or land.

Truth is, anyone with a modicum of interest can grow anything indoors any time. Yes, that means you!

Let There be Light!

Chapter 2

One of the first indoor gardeners I ever met gave me this bit of folksy wisdom: "Ain't no plants growin' in caves." I guess he's probably right. Even if some plants are able to grow in caves they're probably about as spectacular as one of those blind cave fish. Which is to say, not very spectacular at all.

Plants just have to have light! At least the gorgeous leafy green kinds do. Without it they can't produce food to sustain themselves and grow. In case you're curious, this is the official formula:

$$\text{PHOTOSYNTHESIS}$$

$$\text{sun} + CO_2 + H_2O + \text{nutrients} = \text{chlorophyll} \begin{array}{c}\text{carbohydrates}\\ \\ \text{oxygen}\end{array} = \text{yum yum yumm...}$$

So, if you plan to grow indoors, you absolutely must provide your plants with plenty of light. And, just as my grandma was extremely particular about which chocolates she selected from her Whitman's Sampler, it turns out that plants, likewise, are somewhat picky about the kind of light they will use to photosynthesize. Although the sun offers a wide spectrum of light, plants really only respond to the blue and red ranges of that light spectrum. As for Grandma, she sought out the orange creams—doing us all a great service if you ask me.

Room to Grow

I have lived in some places reminiscent of caves. If I had known then what I know now, I could've enjoyed a glorious indoor garden in any one of them. If you have a basement, extra room, or even part of the kitchen to spare, you can successfully play Mother Nature indoors—especially when the weather outside is soul-crushingly gloomy.

What wattage and lighting types you'll need really depend on the amount of space you have to devote to your indoor garden and what sorts of plants you want to grow.

Remember, you'll still need space for your bed, your clothes, the TV, the cat...

Fluorescents & Beyond...

Although they have always been tried-and-true for coaxing my seeds into seedlings, my full spectrum fluorescent tubes were designed to simulate noonday summer sun. I'm afraid they don't do much more than simulate. Typically I leave them on all the time about two inches over the seedbed until the tiny plants start bumping their heads. Then, if I've timed things about right, I can harden them off outside and let Mother Nature take over.

With a little prayer and about fifty more sets of tubes packed into the area, I could, technically, grow my seedlings to maturity inside with my old fluorescents. Now there are newer full spectrum fluorescent systems that produce even more light than my old tubes do, but light intensity still really matters, too.

Unlike fluorescents, a High Intensity Discharge (HID) lamp will offer plants light of the proper spectrum and intensity to carry them from the seedling stage all the way to "Hey, is that a real tomato? It's beautiful!"

I start my seeds in late December or early January under fluorescents and then I switch to HID until the real Mother Nature permits me to plant them outdoors. Of course, there are people who use HID lamps throughout the summer to avoid the extra weeding, the bugs, the heat. . . But I happen to like those things!

Anatomy of a Light System

HID lamps generate light by passing electricity through highly pressurized gas contained in a tube. The kind of gas in the tube and the coating on the bulb determine the spectrum of light emitted. To work, every HID system needs a ballast (the boxy part that contains a power transformer and capacitor) and a socket, which connects to a reflector (the hang-y down part where the bulb goes.) Ranging from 100 watts to 1000, HID lamps come in lots of sizes.

Light for Spinach, Lettuce & other Leafy Greens

If it's mostly vegetative growth you're after—you know, an extra Buttercrunchy lettuce or particularly eye-popping sweet basil—metal halide lighting is the type of HID lighting you need. Similar to the sun's rays in spring and summer, metal halide lamps produce light which is mostly in the blue range of the light spectrum—that's where the eye-popping basil comes in.

Metal halide lights come in all kinds of sizes. Lamps that are just 250 watts and even smaller are available, but you might come to regret choosing these sizes. Small wattage lamps are not usually as energy efficient as larger ones, and you'll be left with a much smaller growing space and less light intensity. Most indoor growers choose 400- or 1000-watt lamps because they provide a lot of light very efficiently. I happen to think 400-watt lamps are just right for starting out.

18

From tomatoes to Chrysanthemums... Light for Fruiting & Flowering!

If you want to encourage your tomato plants to fruit indoors, you'll want to use a high pressure sodium lamp. By emitting light from the red-orange region of the spectrum, this sort of HID lighting simulates the sun's light in fall. Plants under a high pressure sodium light think its time to hurry up and finish their growing cycles so they make flowers and fruit.

People lucky enough to have their own greenhouses sometimes supplement the sun's light with high pressure sodium lamps to promote blooming. But standard high pressure sodium all by itself is not really suited to promoting overall vegetative growth indoors because it lacks the blue part of the light spectrum. For that reason, some gardeners use both metal halide and high pressure sodium types of HID lighting simultaneously. Others encourage green growth with metal halide and then finish with high pressure sodium.

As with metal halides, high pressure sodium lights are available in many different wattages, and, again, lamps that are 250 watts and smaller are not as energy efficient and will not provide the greatest coverage or light intensity. Most greenhouse growers use 400, 600, and 1000 watts because they are among the most energy efficient.

The Best of Both Worlds

Obviously your indoor plants would love to have plenty of blue- and red-spectrum light, but that doesn't mean you have to have two different lighting systems just to suit them. There are a couple of ways you can give them what they want without going broke.

If you have a metal halide light, you can get a special high pressure sodium conversion bulb that will run in your system and put out red spectrum light. That means you can start plants under a standard metal halide lamp and then put in a high pressure sodium bulb when it's time for fruiting and flowering. On the other hand, if you have a high pressure sodium lamp, you can use a metal halide conversion bulb in your system to emit light from the blue part of the spectrum.

Because the conversion process itself takes some energy to accomplish, conversion bulbs aren't quite as efficient as regular metal halide or high pressure sodium bulbs, but they will give you the best of both worlds with just one light system.

Another good option is the two-way ballast. (In case you forget, the ballast is the boxy part that contains the power transformer and capacitor.) Two-way ballasts can actually be switched back and forth depending on your needs at the time. If you want a metal halide lamp, you put in a regular metal halide bulb and switch the ballast to its metal halide setting. For high pressure sodium, you put in a regular high pressure sodium bulb and switch the ballast to the high pressure sodium setting. Pretty neat!

What I Learned in Remedial Science & What's a Lumen Anyway?

If only I had taken my father's advanced life science class in the eighth grade, I might be towering in the field of helioseismology by now. But because I was too embarrassed to have my father as my teacher, I insisted on taking science from a different instructor. Unfortunately, the only alternative that would work with my schedule was the remedial science class—during which the class thugs pelted me with Skittles and carved their initials into the desktops. Needless to say, I didn't learn much. To this day, math and science are not my strongest subjects, but I understand just enough about lumens—the measure of light intensity—to make indoor gardening work.

Since the late 1800s committees of incredibly smart people from all over the world have gotten together to create and agree upon units and standards of mass, electricity, photometry, temperature, and much more. We can thank them for the host of oddly named units of measurement including the henry and the becquerel—along with plenty you've probably heard of: amps, volts, ohms, and joules to name a few. We can thank them for the lumen, too.

Lumen is Latin for "light" and one lumen looks something like this:

1 foot

21

If you were to light a candle, step one foot away, and then measure the amount of light given off by the candle in a one-square-foot section, the measurable light in that section would equal one lumen. As a helpful point of reference, your standard 60-watt incandescent bulb has a light output of about 840 lumens and a 75-watt bulb has a light output of about 1170 lumens. Each of my 40-watt fluorescent tubes puts out 2250 lumens, and some of the new compact fluorescent systems can emit nearly 8,000 lumens. In comparison, one 1000-watt high pressure sodium bulb can produce a whopping 140,000 lumens!

What Wattage?

Maybe by now you've decided where you want your indoor garden to be. The size of that area will determine the number and size of the plants you can grow and what HID wattage to use. Most plants like at least 25 watts per square foot of garden space so a lamp that is 175 watts or less covers about four square feet. When you step up to a 250-watt light, you can cover roughly nine square feet. A 400-watt lamp will light 16 square feet, and, if you have an even larger indoor garden, you could use 600 to 1000 watts to cover 40 to 100 square feet.

Spacing & Lumens

Spacing your plants properly is a little like choosing the right puppy. Sure, this one is so cute with his tiny nose and floppy ears, but will he fit in the house once he has grown? You wouldn't want to start a whole flat of tomatoes if you'll only have room for three or four mature plants within your light coverage area. If your reflector hangs at least a foot away from the ceiling and your plants are at least one foot off the floor, that leaves about four to six feet of space in which your plants can grow. As such, it's important to think about how big they will get when they have matured.

Something else to consider? The closer your plants are to the light, the more lumens they will get. In other words, a lamp placed high above your plants will spread less intense light over a large area, and a lamp placed close to your plants will provide more intense light over a smaller area. Want to grow low-light plants such as lettuce? You wouldn't need to place them too close to the light. Want to grow sun-loving plants such as sunflowers? You would want to place them much closer.

If you want to get really fancy, you can calculate the intensity of light your plants receive with this formula:

$$\text{Light intensity} = \text{Total available Lumens} \div (\text{Distance})^2$$

If you play around with the formula a little you would notice that light intensity really falls off as you go farther away from the light source. But, don't worry, you can always avoid the math and just eyeball things to gauge whether or not your plants are getting what they need. Plants that look really lanky with weak, long stems may be too far from your light source. Plants that look a bit crispy are much too close. Contented plants will show compact, uniform growth.

If you have a low-watt system, you can place your plants fairly close to the light without the danger of scorching them, but you should be more careful with higher wattages. The hand rule is a good one to follow. If you put your hand under the lamp above the canopy of your plants and it feels too hot for you, that distance is probably also too hot for your plants. Make sense?

Usually, smaller HIDs are placed six to 12 inches above the garden, 400-watt bulbs go 18 to 24 inches above plants, and 600- and 1000-watt lights work well 24 to 36 inches above the plant canopy.

If you have more than one HID lamp running at once or if you are running a 600-watt system or larger, you may find that conditions in your indoor garden can get fairly hot and humid. Some gardeners use special reflector vents to pull hot air away from their lamps. Oscillating fans help, too.

Finally, the light coming from the center of the reflector is the most intense so plants in the center of the growing area may begin to dominate those on the fringes. Switch the plants in the center with those on the outer edges every now and then to even things out. And, as plants grow, you should space them further apart so that they don't shade one another.

Watt am I Paying?

When I go to the local nursery it's nothing for me to spend 75 bucks—even though I had budgeted $35. It's the kind of place that makes those charming little red wagons available to customers like me. I grab a rosemary, a few Echinacea, some peppers, tomatoes, butterfly bush. . . One by one the four-inch pots add up and suddenly my red wagon is bursting with stuff.

If you have a habit like mine, you'll probably find that HID lighting eventually pays for itself because you'll no longer need to spend a fortune on commercial bedding plants each year. A medium-sized system can cost a few hundred dollars and running HID lighting will increase your monthly electricity bill from $5 to $50 depending on the wattage and number of hours you use.

This should give you a better idea of what to expect:

Light size	Per hour cost	Each 12-hour day	Per month
250 watt	.0175	.21	$6.30
400 watt	.028	.336	$10.08
600 watt	.042	.504	$15.12
1000 watt	.07	.84	$25.20

This little chart isn't a hard-and-fast rule. (I based these estimates on a cost of seven cents per kilowatt hour.) You should check your electric bill to determine your local kilowatt hour cost to get a better idea of your operating costs.

25

There are a few ways you can make sure you and your plants are getting your money's worth. The first is to be certain your bulb is performing at its peak. Most HID lamps will continue to light beyond 18 months of use, but they will have lost up to 30 percent or more of their lumen output while consuming the same amount of electricity! You can expect metal halide bulbs to last up to 12,000 hours while high pressure sodium bulbs have a life expectancy of up to 24,000 hours. As a general rule, replace metal halide bulbs every 10 to 15 months and replace high pressure sodium bulbs every 18 to 24 months. Don't forget to let your reflector and bulb cool completely before replacing it. If you aren't sure whether or not your bulb has lost a few lumens along the way, you can also use a light meter to check its strength.

Have you seen sun worshippers on the beach holding those weird-looking metal reflector sheets underneath their faces to bounce light back up under their chins? Shiny light reflective material such as Mylar works like that in the indoor garden by redirecting light that might otherwise be wasted. (Of course, your plants need not worry about skin cancer . . .)

Light movers can further maximize your plants' use of light. Typically used in very large grow rooms, mechanized light movers guide HID lamps along a track so that all of the plants get equal exposure to light.

Timing is Everything!

Depending on what you want to grow and when you want to grow it, you may need this: The duration of light plants receive is just as important as the type and intensity of light Mother Nature offers. Depending on the length of the days and nights, plants seem to know which part of their life cycles they should be working on. If you think about some of the plants you regularly grow outdoors, you'll come to recognize that one plant's photoperiod—the special relationship between periods of light and darkness—may not be the same as another's. When do your tomatoes flower and fruit? Midsummer when the days are long and nights are short. What about flowers that only come up in the spring or the fall? Flowers such as perennial asters require longer periods of darkness to signal flowering. That's why you won't see them flowering outdoors in the middle of summer.

Plants in a vegetative growth stage like about 18 hours of light per day. By contrast, most plants need 12 hours of uninterrupted darkness to flower. If they don't get this, they will simply hang out in their vegetative growth stage. That means if you want to get things to bloom in the middle of winter, you'll have to be mindful of photoperiods. You can coax them into flowering by giving them 10 to 12 hours of red-spectrum light with a corresponding lights-off period.

By using a timer with your HID lamp, you can exactly control your indoor seasons. If you do decide to try a timer, choose one that's grounded and be sure it offers the adequate amperage and power rating to meet your needs.

Just so you know, an amp is a unit measuring the strength of an electric current; that's where the word "amperage" comes from. If you have 20 amps available to you in a circuit and

By the way, if you want to work on your plants in the garden room during their Lights-off phase, you can use a GREEN incandescent bulb so that you won't disturb the plants while they're resting!

your HID lamp draws 15 amps, it wouldn't be a good idea to try running your hair dryer in the same circuit at the same time. You would most likely overload the circuit and blow a fuse. Know the electrical load your circuits can take, and pay attention to the number of amps your lights, timers, fans, and other equipment will use. Because I like to leave some wiggle room for bizarre power surges, I only use about 80 percent of the amps available to me per circuit.

The How-to Part

If you live in an apartment or house with updated wiring, you probably have ground fault interrupt outlets. Those are recommended for indoor gardens, but, whether you have them or not, I insist that you get a surge-protected power strip with an on-off switch before you do much else. Also, if your indoor garden will be in a finished room with carpet or a nice, hardwood floor, you should protect it with a heavy sheet of plastic before getting busy with pots and plants.

No matter what kind of system you've decided on, you'll want to keep your ballast high and dry off the floor. Mine has its very own shelf just to keep it up and out of harm's way. As for the reflector, mount it with sturdy, weight-bearing hooks and chain. Leave at least a foot of space between the top of the reflector and the spot from which you've chosen to hang it. (In my case, that's the ceiling.)

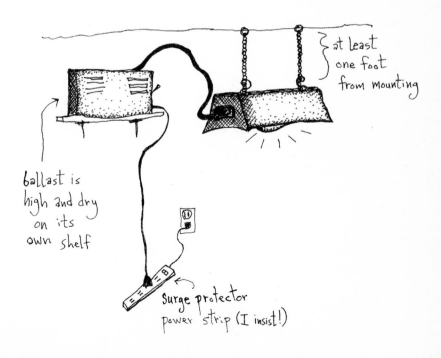

at least
one foot
from mounting

ballast is
high and dry
on its
own shelf

Surge protector
power strip (I insist!)

Once the reflector is securely in place, you can screw in the proper bulb. Always double check to make sure you are using the right wattage and type (metal halide or high pressure sodium) for your system first! Typically, I clean the bulb with a clean, dry cloth before screwing it into the socket. Once the bulb is in place, check it closely one more time. Do you see any oily marks or fingerprints on its surface? Because bulbs that are squeaky-clean are more efficient than those that aren't, you should very carefully clean off any oily residue you notice before proceeding. Again, a clean, dry cloth—without any fancy cleaning solution—is all you need for the job.

Now it's time to insert the safety lens. This is a pane of tempered glass with beveled edges that slides into a track along the bottom edge of the reflector hood. Some reflectors have extra clamps to further secure the safety lens. As with your bulb, the lens should be very clean and dry and you'll need to check it for smudges and clean them up one last time before you move on.

Next you should plug your surge-protected power strip into your electrical outlet. Make sure the power strip is in the "OFF" position. Now plug the reflector cord into your ballast and then plug the ballast cord into the power strip. From now on you'll turn your lamp off or on via the switch on your power strip.

If you're really excited, you can go ahead and switch on your light just to see what happens. It will take about five minutes to get going, and it won't seem that bright at first, but, trust me, the light output becomes increasingly spectacular!

Because of the large amount of voltage required to power up, you should turn your light system on only once a day. Also, the more you turn your light on and off, the faster your bulb will burn out. If you do have to restart your lamp for any reason, wait at least 15 minutes first so that it has a chance to cool completely.

And, speaking of cooling, you should know that higher wattage lamps can put off a fair amount of heat. You can keep your ballast—and your plants—from getting too hot with an oscillating fan.

Bzzzzpt!

They say curiosity killed the cat, but satisfaction brought him back. I say if that cat doesn't respect electricity, no amount of satisfaction can unfry his fur.

I have paid a premium trying to satisfy my natural sense of curiosity. As a child, I once kissed a 100-watt light bulb that had already been on for about four hours. I burned my lips and tongue. It was my first real kiss.

I have been known to stick butter knives in the toaster just to see what happens.

Not to sound like your mother, but I want you to be safe while you enjoy your indoor garden! Here are a few things to watch:

- Never plug your ballast cord directly into your home outlet. Use a grounded power strip instead. (Plug the power strip into the outlet, ballast into the power strip, and then switch on the power strip.)

- If you must use an extension cord, use only the heavy duty kind, and, because extension cords are not equipped with circuit breakers, never, ever plug an extension cord directly into your ballast.

- Don't stand in puddles or have wet hands when plugging in or switching on your system. My friend Peggy got the shock of her life when she plugged in her small fluorescents with damp hands. Imagine what a 1000-watt HID lamp could do!

- Don't touch the ballast when it's on.

- Never try to clean your bulb while it's on. It will shatter. Promise.

- You don't stare at the sun regularly and you certainly shouldn't stare into your bulb—especially if it has broken while the system is in use. In that case, turn off the lamp right away and wait at least 15 minutes for the system and what's left of your bulb to cool completely before replacing it.

Down & Dirty: Soil Gardening Indoors

Chapter 3

Ever tried to grow radishes in New Orleans swamp muck? It was the sixth-grade science fair, and, while so many of my colleagues were captivated by the more glamorous erupting volcano demonstrations, I, naturally, chose to get my hands dirty.

I asked a helicopter pilot I knew to collect soil samples for my experiment, and as a result, I had specimens from Indiana, Texas, Oklahoma, and, yes, Louisiana. To see how well plants could grow in different soil types, I started radish seeds in each sample, carefully affording each the same amount of water and light.

It probably comes as no surprise that the Texas sample—especially rich and well draining—outperformed the others growing a radish so ravishing I had to testify that I had not given it any special treatment. As for the Louisiana sample? Its radish was tragically spindly.

Anyway, most gardeners know that healthy plant growth is dependent upon soil quality, of course, but not everyone understands just what makes some soils so much more productive than others. Get that part down and you can't help but have a wildly productive indoor garden.

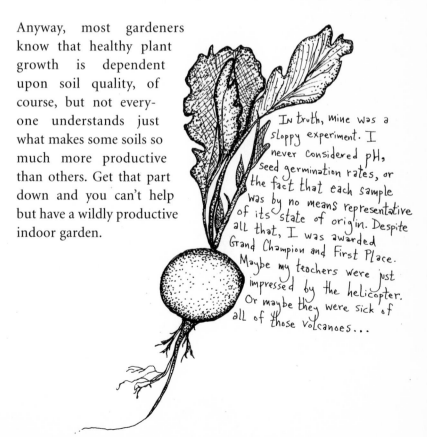

In truth, mine was a sloppy experiment. I never considered pH, seed germination rates, or the fact that each sample was by no means representative of its state of origin. Despite all that, I was awarded Grand Champion and First Place. Maybe my teachers were just impressed by the helicopter. Or maybe they were sick of all of those volcanoes...

It's Alive!

Animal, mineral, or vegetable? In a sense, healthy soil is made up of all three. Soil contains decaying animals and plants as well as tiny bits of rock—but soil is also very much alive. Packed tighter than the New York subway, soil contains billions of living organisms including insects, worms, and bacteria as well as soil fungi and algae. They may not know it, but they all work together to convert organic matter into nutrients our plants can use.

Soil Structure

The right soil structure is also especially important for indoor growing because roots have to be able to breathe and easily access water and nutrients. If the soil you provide your plants is too heavy and compacted, their roots will have to work much harder than is really necessary to push through it. Heavy clay soils are made up of very small, tightly packed particles, making them neither well aerated nor easily penetrated. Your soil can also be too loose. Sandy soils contain much larger particles so they afford roots plenty of air and allow them to penetrate the soil easily, but they do not retain water very well. Also, soil that is too loose can't adequately support a large, heavy plant such as a tomato.

Most plants prefer soil that is a bit crumbly. Just-right, silt soils contain medium-sized particles that provide good drainage and aeration. You may think you have just the right type of soil in your garden outdoors. Still, you should resist digging up outdoor soil for your indoor garden because you'd be bringing in insect pests, harmful bacteria, and plant diseases along with it.

Some indoor gardeners go so far as to sanitize their outdoor soil by baking it in an oven. Baking a small pan of soil on 175°F for about 30 minutes is said to eliminate harmful nematodes, damping-off disease, soil insects, most plant viruses, and most weed seeds.

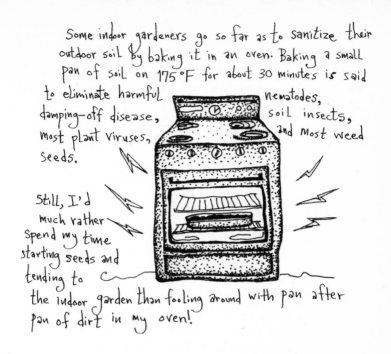

Still, I'd much rather spend my time starting seeds and tending to the indoor garden than fooling around with pan after pan of dirt in my oven!

For the most successful soil gardening indoors, your best bet is mixing your own growing medium. My preferred soil mix includes equal parts of store-bought, organic topsoil, worm castings, and vermiculite. I mix each ingredient very thoroughly by hand in a large plastic bin.

By the way, the term "worm castings" is, essentially, a nice way of saying "worm poop." Also known as vermicompost, worm castings make a terrific, non-alkaline fertilizer that is high in natural nutrients and beneficial microorganisms. You can order large quantities of worm castings from commercial worm farms or you can make your own by starting a worm pile. (See appendix for more information on vermicomposting!)

By mixing your own growing medium, you can make special adjustments to suit the needs of specific plants. For instance, do you want to grow plants that love heavier soils? For a richer, moister growing environment, give heavy-soil plants such as bleeding hearts, bee balm, and foxglove extra worm castings and shredded coconut fiber (a by-product of the coconut industry, shredded, compressed coconut shell fiber is now being used with great success as a soil amendment because it is extremely absorbent), or vermiculite. If, on the other hand, you need a well-draining soil mix, you can add coarse sand or perlite to create a drier growing environment.

Mycorrhiza is perhaps the most magical ingredient in my indoor soil mix. I add mycorrhizal fungal spores to help protect plant roots from harmful bacteria and problem fungi. The fine threads of mycorrhizal fungi also help plants maximize nutrient uptake by attaching to plant roots, seeking out water and nutrients, then funneling them both back to the plant. Be advised, this stuff isn't cheap, but it is well worth trying. I use granulated mycorrhizal inoculant on my perennial herbs and flowers.

One soil amendment that is great for the outdoor garden but not so great indoors is compost. You should avoid using it in your indoor soil mix because it can harbor soil-borne disease. You may also be tempted to reuse your soil mix after a growing cycle is finished. This, too, is a bad idea. As with compost, undesirable fungi and microorganisms can grow in old soil mix. Used soil mix is, however, a fine amendment for the outdoor garden.

 Tiny Seeds: Big Miracles!

My favorite part of indoor gardening is seed starting, and, after all these years, the process still amazes me. I wonder how my eight-foot-tall sunflower, its leaves the size of dinner plates, could possibly have sprung from a seed no larger than my fingernail. Or the thick maze of heirloom tomato plants that exploded out of what was once just a handful of pale, flat seeds.

For me, seed starting is not only mesmerizing but also very practical because, for what it costs to buy a few flats of bedding plants, I can grow many, many more plants from seed. And, rather than settle for whatever plant varieties the nursery decided to start in the spring, I can grow rare strains of herbs and vegetables—as long as I can find seed stock for them! The best part of all is being certain that they had the healthiest possible start.

I must know, if you've never started your own seeds or rooted cuttings indoors, what on earth have you been waiting for? It's easy, and, if you are to have any sort of garden in the middle of winter— when all the nurseries have closed for the season—you'll need to know how to propagate plants.

If this is OLD HAT to you, skip ahead. It's really OK with me...

Besides seeds, of course, you've got to have a good growing medium. Seeds come with their own food supply so you don't have to start them in your soil mixture right away. In fact, it's better if you start them—as well as any cuttings you make—in an inert, well-draining medium. I have had great success with expandable peat pots and specialized starter plugs. I like those best because once your plant has established its roots, you can just chuck the whole thing into the ground or, in the case of your indoor garden, your container.

One thing to keep in mind about peat pots: they can wick moisture away from your plants...

Commercially prepared seedling mixes with perlite are good, too, but they will dry out more quickly because they're so lightweight. If you are a little on the lazy side (me!) and you aren't always as on top of your watering schedule as you'd like (me again!), I recommend starting your seeds in straight coconut fiber.

The coconut fiber I've used came in a large brick. A friend of mine turned me on to these, and they are pretty cool. He said, "Take it home and put it in a bucket of water. Leave it there for about 15 minutes. It will absorb most of the water and get really, really big." So, feeling kind of silly, I put the brick in my bucket of water and went away for a while. I didn't actually expect it to work, but when I came back, it had expanded so much that it was peeking out of the top of my bucket! Needless to say, it holds water really well.

As for the growing containers, durable plastic cells and flats work well. I like to use mine again and again and again until they fall apart. I clean them with one part non-chlorine bleach to ten parts water in between uses to protect my new seedlings from disease that may have gotten started during my last round of seed starting. If you decide to do this, make sure you rinse your flats really well and dry them completely before using them again. Clay pots and peat pots are other options, but both can wick moisture away from your plants' roots.

This may sound silly, but, when you sow your seeds, don't forget to label them! The last time I thought I could get away with skipping this step I lost track of everything. Like newborns, seedlings look pretty much the same to me. I did my best to sort them all out— only to watch my yellow squash turn into a cantaloupe. And, to this day, I'm still not sure what became of the watermelons. Did I ever even plant them in the first place? Well, anyway, I've learned my lesson, and now I use little wooden stakes labeled with permanent marker to remind me what's where.

Now, more than anything seeds like it warm. Most seeds started indoors germinate at a temperature of 70–75° F. Because they usually raise the temperature of your growing medium by about 10 degrees, seedling heat mats make a great secret weapon for hard-to-start plants like lavender. Overall, they are great for speeding up the germination process, and they offer cuttings additional protection against transplant shock.

Clear plastic domes that fit over the tops of your flats can also be used to trap heat and moisture within your growing medium, but be careful. Covered seedlings can get too much moisture so you'll want to uncover them now and then to give them some fresh air.

When sowing your seeds you may be tempted to really pack them in. Resist that temptation. Not only are they more susceptible to disease, seeds planted too close to one another must compete for available light and space.

Unless your seeds require light to germinate as indicated on their package, cover your seeds very lightly with more growing medium, keep the whole tray moist, and—the hardest part—be patient. Once your seedlings are up, you'll want to remove any propagation heat mats and humidity domes you may have used and add plenty of light.

If your seedlings don't get enough light, they'll start to look leggier than the Rockettes. For vigorous, compact growth, expose them to eight to ten hours of light daily and remember to turn the lights off at night to replicate their natural cycle as if they were growing outdoors.

Use an oscillating fan near your seedlings to stir the air. This will help them to grow stronger stems.

Your seedlings have plenty to eat until they get their "true leaves." Those are the second set of leaves that grow from the plant's stem. Once a seedling has its true leaves, it needs additional energy in the way of nutrients so it's time to transplant them into larger containers of your soil mix. For the very best results, choose containers that are taller than they are wide. Containers with square bottoms are particularly suited for indoor gardeners with tiny spaces because they can be placed right next to one another if you like. During this growth period, keep the soil medium moist—but not waterlogged!—and fertilize as needed.

How to take Cuttings

As you surely know, some plants are more stubborn than others, and you'll have more success taking cuttings of an established plant than trying to coax them to life from seed. Herbaceous plants like rosemary and thyme come to mind.

Plants rooted from cuttings are also known as "clones" because they exhibit properties identical to their parent plants. To root plant cuttings you need some basic supplies including a very clean, sharp knife and your inert, soilless growing medium. Since cuttings can be a little persnickety, I also count propagation heat mats and root-promoting gels among my basic supplies because they really do increase the number of cuttings that successfully root.

In particular, root-promoting gels help prevent transplant shock and spur growth because they contain rooting hormone, vitamins, and minerals that cuttings can use in a pinch. Most root promoters come in powder, gel, and liquid forms. Don't bother with powders; they can easily wash off of your cuttings. I prefer gels because they actually seal the plant's exposed root surface—protecting it from air bubbles and contaminants. You can take extra precautions by using root-promoting liquids in conjunction with gels, but I think the gels work well enough by themselves.

To take cuttings, choose only the healthiest plants and be very gentle. Select a stem that has two or three leaf sets and locate a spot on the branch next to a set of leaf nodes (the points where leaves grow out of the stem) where you will make a clean 45-degree slice. Leave at least one node set above your cut and remove the lower one or two sets of leaves—these are the points from which new roots will grow. You need at least one good set of leaves and you can trim remaining sets of leaves as needed. (Plants lose moisture through their leaves so by reducing the number of leaves, you help them to conserve water!)

(Remove leaf and branch here, too!)

Cut Stem at 45° angle...

Leaf Node... (Remove leaf and branch here!)

Now you can apply a root promoter if you want, but don't lollygag! To survive, your cuttings need to be placed directly into your moistened growing medium right away. Keep humidity levels high by covering cuttings with a clear plastic dome and keep them out of direct sunlight until healthy roots are established.

When I got really good at taking cuttings I found myself faced with an ethical dilemma. See, I live near a university with great landscaping, and it is all I can do not to creep into their expanses of ivy and stands of lavender, scissors and plastic bags in hand, and snip! snip! two inches off the top here and there to secret the cuttings away for my own stock. Is it stealing? Or some weird kind of preservation? Am I a plant bandit? Will I go to Gardening Hell?...

Gardening without Soil? Oh Yes!

Chapter 4

If you've ever grown ivy or rooted an avocado in a jar of water, you've already experimented with passive hydroponics. I've had the same philodendron growing in a small bottle of plain water for several years now. Originally, the bottle was to be but a temporary home, but I came to enjoy watching the thick, white roots grow down, slightly magnified by the water. After a few months of this I realized I would probably never bother potting up my plant at all. How long could it live like that? The roots spiraled around and around inside the bottle. I only had to top off the water as it evaporated and say a few encouraging words now and then, and it grew and grew, cascading down the side of the bottle, over my desk, down to the floor. . . It is still growing.

Hydroponics aptly means "working water." No soil is used in hydroponics. Instead, plants are supported in inert growing media like those used for seed starting or the propagation of cuttings, and plant roots have direct access to nutrient-infused water.

If you don't have much space in which to grow, hydroponics is a very good indoor gardening solution. Plants grown hydroponically seem to know there is plenty of plant food to go around so they don't have to fight one another for access to nutrients. Moreover, they never get too much or too little water so all they need occupy themselves with is growing.

When growing it outside would be inconceivable because of extreme heat or cold, I grow my lettuce and spinach in a hydroponics system indoors. They seem to grow in double-time! And they aren't usually troubled with pests or soil-borne diseases—unless I accidentally bring them in from the outdoors on my clothes or shoes. Oops! Also, since there aren't weed seeds hiding in my growing medium, my plants never have to share their space—not to mention available nutrients—with weeds.

If you've never dabbled with hydroponics before, but you think you want to, try starting with basil or peppers. I think you'll be very pleased with the results. Nearly anything you might wish to grow—cucumbers, snow peas, sunflowers, tomatoes, small fruit trees, roses, whatever!—will do wonderfully well without soil!

Growing Media: We all Need a Little Support

But, if your plants won't be growing in soil, just what exactly will they be growing in? Really, any inert material that can physically support the plant will do. Choosing which one to use is a bit like choosing a really good pair of pantyhose. Too much support and you feel you're being simultaneously strangled and crushed. Too little and you're flopping around all over the place. The same is true for hydroponically grown plants. Some hydroponic gardeners use coarse river sand, pea gravel, or—in the case of lettuce or other delicate crown plants—very fine perlite depending on how much or how little support they need.

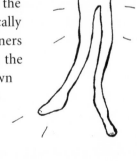

Another natural medium hydro growers use is compressed coconut fiber. You may remember loose, shredded coconut fiber is a popular soil amendment, but coconut fiber is also used in hydroponics. For that application, the coconut material comes in washed, pressed slabs or cubes. Of all the types of hydroponic growing media, coconut fiber is certainly one of the most absorbent. If you like, after you've used coconut fiber in a hydroponics system, you can shred it and use it to amend your soil outdoors.

Rockwool and expanded clay pellets are a couple of man-made growing media that are widely used. Rockwool is spun glass wool made of volcanic rock. It looks and feels like steel wool, and it comes in all shapes and sizes. For me, rockwool has a couple of drawbacks. First, to reduce the chance that the pH of this medium will react with that of your nutrient solution, you have to pre-soak rockwool for at least 24 hours before using it, and I am just not that patient. Also, rockwool cubes and slabs are neither easily reused, nor biodegradable. I don't like the idea of filling up our landfills with rockwool when some other method would do! Nevertheless, rockwool does offer good plant support and retains air and moisture incredibly well. To lock in extra moisture, some hydroponic gardeners top their rockwool with shredded coconut fiber.

Unlike rockwool, expanded clay pellets won't react with your nutrient solution and are easy to reuse crop after crop. Also, they will provide plenty of airspace so your plant roots stay healthy and oxygen-rich. (Can you tell they are my favorite?) The porous clay pebbles come in different sizes—large for larger plants like tomatoes and cucumbers, medium for, say, peppers or mid-size flowers, and small for delicate crown plants—and they even come in different colors, just for fun. Just be sure you pick the right size, OK? The first time I grew lettuce in a hydroponics system, I made the mistake of using expanded clay pellets that were too big. I had to be extra careful when working around my plants when they were still very small because the large balls would roll right over the tops of them!

Whatever soilless growing medium you choose, it must afford your plant roots plenty of moisture and oxygen—and it must be able to work with the type of hydroponics method you wish to try.

Passive and Active Plant Pampering

Because they require no moving parts, passive hydroponics systems are cheap, portable, and easy to set up. The wick method is probably the most common type of passive hydroponics and works like this:

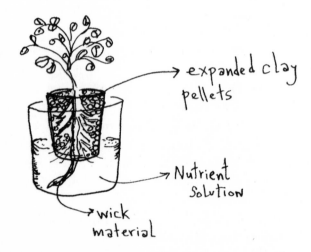

In a wick system, your plants are anchored in an inert growing medium such as vermiculite, perlite, shredded coconut fiber, soilless mix, or expanded clay pellets and an absorbent material—usually thick rope or cloth—extends from the plants' root zone to the nutrient reservoir. Without the use of pumps or electricity, the absorbent material or wick naturally draws nutrients from the solution to the plant roots. All you have to do is make sure that the nutrient reservoir stays full!

Because your plants won't get as much oxygen to their roots as they'd like, you can't expect super-accelerated plant growth from a wick system. Passive hydroponics is pretty neat if you've never known anything else, but be warned: once you've tried one of the active methods, I doubt you'll want to go back!

Plants grown in active hydroponics systems are fed breakfast in bed. Active systems pump nutrient-rich solution directly to the plant root zone. Some common active hydroponics methods are the continuous aeration technique (CAT), ebb and flow, drip, aeroponics, and the nutrient film technique (NFT).

I have had great luck with the continuous aeration technique, and it is a good method to start out with. My system looks like this:

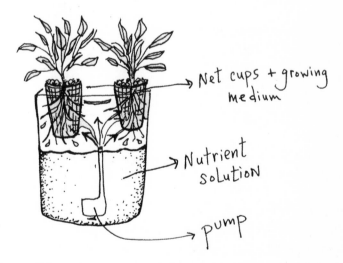

A submersible pump is suctioned to the bottom of my reservoir such that it continually splashes nutrient solution up onto my plant roots which grow down through net cups. This simple action ensures the nutrient solution is well-oxygenated and always available to plants. Pea gravel, coconut fiber, and, yes, expanded clay pellets work best in these kinds of systems.

If you've heard of them at all, you may have heard ebb and flow systems referred to as "flood and drain" systems. That's just what they do.

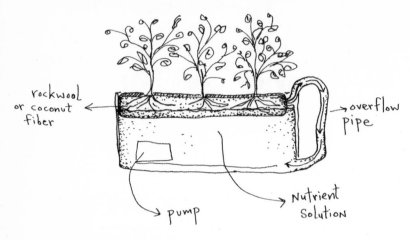

In ebb and flow systems, plant roots are supported in slabs, cubes, or blocks of coconut fiber or rockwool that are periodically flooded with nutrient solution. Once the solution has reached a set level, an overflow pipe drains the excess back into the main reservoir. As the cycles of flooding and draining are repeated, oxygen-rich air is regularly pushed straight to your plants' roots. This increases their ability to take in nutrients and grow.

With the drip method, a submersible pump is placed in the nutrient solution reservoir and individual supply lines drip solution to the roots of each plant like this:

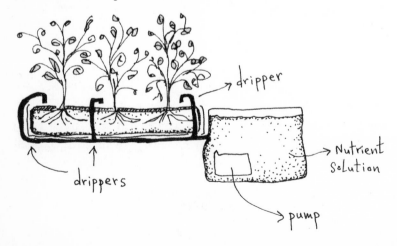

Plants are best anchored in rockwool or coconut fiber slabs, but expanded clay pellets or soilless mix will work, too. If you like, you can recirculate the leftover nutrient solution, but make sure that your supply lines don't get clogged.

Talk about pampered! For plants, I think growing in an aeroponics system is just about as good as it gets. It must be a little like going to a spa. Here's how it works:

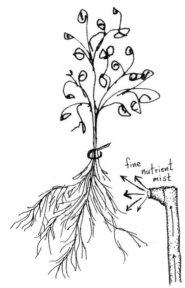

fine nutrient mist

Plants can be suspended without any growing medium at all or they can be grown in net cups filled with expanded clay pellets. Plant roots are sprayed directly with a fine nutrient- and oxygen-rich mist so they are constantly moist and aerated at the same time. With this nearly unlimited access to oxygen, roots have maximum potential to absorb nutrients and your plants—and especially cuttings—zoom along.

Be aware that aeroponics does require greater attention to detail because the delicate sprayer nozzles must be kept free of debris or they can clog. Also, if you have problems with your equipment or if you have a power failure, you can lose all of your plants in no time because they've come to depend on the royal treatment.

Because newer, better technology has replaced it, the nutrient film technique isn't quite as widespread as it once was, but you may still come across it. As with aeroponics, little or no soilless medium is used. Instead, plants are supported in rockwool, coconut fiber slabs, or expanded clay pellets over channels of an air-permeable film of nutrient. The nutrient solution is continually and rapidly pumped over the plant roots to the end of the growing channel. Then it drains back down into the main reservoir where it is pumped back up to the start of the growing channel. If you plan to use an NFT system, remember that they are also susceptible to clogs, and, because plants are so vulnerable, power failure can spell sudden death for your plants.

If you are even sort of handy, you can make your own customized hydroponics system. Inexpensive materials such as PVC pipe, plastic hose, and 10-gallon buckets can be combined with small pumps to create your own ebb and flow, aeroponics, and drip systems, to name a few.

One very easy and inexpensive system to build requires two large buckets—one inside of the other—and a small pump.

You can grow a large plant (maybe a banana tree!) in coconut fiber, expanded clay pellets, or soilless mix in the inner bucket while the outer bucket serves as the nutrient solution reservoir. The solution, delivered via the pump to the top bucket, trickles down through the root system and out drainage holes back into the nutrient reservoir.

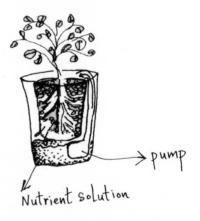

> pump

Nutrient solution

If you want to grow lots of plants in a small space on the cheap, start with a framework of large-diameter plastic piping. To create the plant sites, drill large holes at regular intervals along the tubing. Plants like basil and lettuce then grow in coconut fiber or expanded clay pellets inside net cups placed in the holes and the roots are constantly bathed in nutrient solution flowing through the tubing.

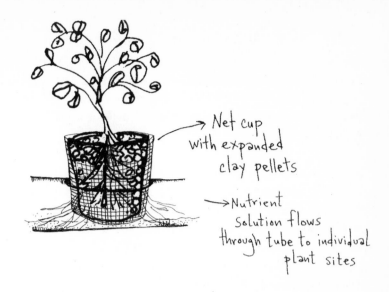

→ Net cup
with expanded
clay pellets

→ Nutrient
Solution flows
through tube to individual
plant sites

Still not sure where to start? One great way
to build your confidence is to modify an existing
hydroponics system to accommodate specific numbers
and types of plants. You can also visit hydroponics
shops to pick a few brains...

Decided which method you want to try? Keep in mind it's a good idea to change the nutrient solution in your reservoir about once a week so your plants stay happy. When you have just finished a growing cycle or you're about to start a new one, completely drain your reservoir, remove any plant debris you can find, and run a light, non-chlorine bleach solution—about an eighth of a cup for every gallon of water—through the system for about half a day. Then, drain your reservoir again and run fresh water through the system to remove any traces of bleach.

Hydroponics in History

Turns out people have been doing without dirt for a very long time. The Hanging Gardens of Babylon, the Egyptians' nutrient-rich irrigation systems, and the Aztecs' Floating Gardens of Xocahimilco are all thought to be precursors to hydroponics.

Out of necessity, hydroponics really took off during World War II when the U.S. Army Air Forces turned a desolate island in the South Pacific into a large-scale hydroponic vegetable farm. It had been impossible to ship fresh lettuce, tomatoes, and other veggies to the troops on Ascension Island, a strategic airfield for U.S. warplanes, so the enlisted men took it upon themselves to grow what they needed on 80,000 square feet of volcanic rock.

W. Robert Moore, 1945

How Do These Cucumbers Compare with Those in Your Victory Garden? All GI's on Ascension agree that food grown by hydroponics is "pretty fine eating!" The sturdy vines are trained on vertical string supports, thus requiring small space in the garden. Plants begin producing 8 to 9 weeks after planting and can be picked continuously for a minimum of about two months.

Food for Plants

Chapter 5

Nuts or not? "Yes" to red wine and "no" to red meat? Just when we think we've figured out what we should or shouldn't eat for better health, scientists and dieticians seem to change the rules on us. Fortunately, we seem to have most of the answers when it comes to feeding our plants. If there were a food pyramid for plants it might look like this:

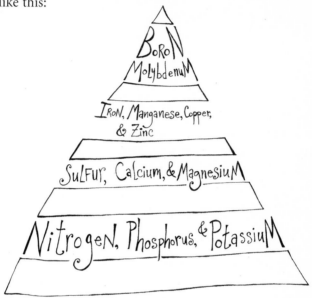

Because plants need nitrogen, phosphorus, and potassium in large amounts, these elements are known as primary macronutrients. Plants require smaller amounts of the secondary macronutrients—sulfur, calcium, and magnesium. Iron, manganese, zinc, copper, chlorine, boron, and molybdenum are still essential for growth but are required in even smaller amounts. They are often referred to as micronutrients or trace elements.

Each of these macro- and micronutrients serves specific purposes for our plants, and, for plants grown indoors, it's entirely up to us to make sure we supply them. In addition to providing a good, all-purpose fertilizer, indoor gardeners need to be on the lookout for nutrient deficiencies. This isn't always easy because different nutrient deficiencies can look similar to one another. What's more, deficiencies in some nutrients may in turn reduce the availability of other nutrients. But don't sweat it. Some of this may sound like brain surgery, but it's really not.

Nitrogen (N)

Nitrogen is always listed first in the fertilizer grade (or N-P-K ratio) on nutrient product bags, boxes, and bottles because it is one of the biggies. (For example, if the ratio on your nutrient package reads "11-13-3", that means it contains 11 percent nitrogen.) Plants use nitrogen to produce new, green growth. Without it, new growth is really stunted and older plant leaves start to turn yellow and die. You'll always want to look for symptoms of nitrogen deficiency in the older leaves first because, when nitrogen is scarce, the new leaves will hit up the old leaves for their nitrogen.

Of course, I've learned the hard way that you can have too much of a good thing. The last time I was heavy-handed with the nitrogen, my tomato plants grew scads of giant, dark green leaves and, unfortunately, that was just about all they accomplished that season.

Phosphorus (P)

Phosphorus, another biggie, is listed second in the N-P-K ratio. (That nutrient package with the "11-13-3" ratio contains 13 percent phosphorus.) Phosphorus is essential to plant fruiting and flowering because it promotes root growth. When you supplement the amount of phosphorus your flowering plants get, you'll likely notice more blooms and more vigorous growth overall. Without enough, though, young plants are slow to grow and mature plants won't really feel like flowering.

66

When plants lack phosphorus, their stems and older leaves often turn yellow and then a sort of reddish-purple. That's because, as with nitrogen deficiency, the new leaves on the block are stealing phosphorus from the old timers.

Potassium (K)

You guessed it. Potassium takes up the last spot in the N-P-K ratio. (So an "11-13-3" nutrient ratio contains 3 percent potassium.) Because plants use potassium to build cells and tissue, supplementing this nutrient contributes to overall plant hardiness. Stronger, more durable plants are usually more tolerant of temperature extremes and are more pest- and disease-resistant.

Think your plants may lack potassium? Watch the older leaves for signs of yellowing between leaf veins. Also, the edges of older leaves may roll up or look burnt.

Sulfur (S)

One of the secondary macronutrients, sulfur helps plants maintain their dark green color. Mainly, plants use sulfur to create essential proteins. You won't see signs of a sulfur deficiency in older leaves because sulfur can't be moved around in plants like some of the other essential nutrients can. If your plants lack sulfur, younger leaves may look yellow and slightly curled. Too much sulfur can cause plants to produce really small leaves.

Calcium (Ca)

Have you ever grown tomatoes with ugly brown spots all over the fruit? Or had tomato blossoms that just died and dropped off? Your plants probably lacked calcium. As with sulfur, plants also need calcium to make proteins.

Calcium promotes new root growth and makes plants super-vigorous. Look for calcium deficiency in young leaves. They will start out deep green and then turn yellow; also, their growth may look distorted.

Magnesium (Mg)

Even though it's classified as a secondary macronutrient, magnesium is still a biggie. Without magnesium, plants can't use light to make food! Plants also need magnesium to be able to take in their other essential nutrients and to make seeds. Signs of magnesium deficiency are similar to those of potassium deficiency. Older leaves will appear yellow between leaf veins, and entire leaves curl. Younger leaves, also, may curl and crumble easily. As magnesium deficiencies progress, older leaves may become mottled with rust-colored spots.

Iron (Fe)

Iron makes for healthy, dark green growth. As with magnesium, iron is essential for photosynthesis. Plants must have iron in order to produce chlorophyll. You'll notice signs of an iron deficiency in new growth because iron—and most of the other micronutrients—cannot be moved around from older leaves to newer ones. If your plants lack iron, new leaves will look very pale. Areas between leaf veins may be bright yellow while the veins themselves stay green. In severe cases, leaves and blossoms may drop off.

Manganese (Mn)

In short, manganese makes things happen. Manganese is necessary for chlorophyll formation, and without it, plants wouldn't be able to carry out essential cellular functions. As with plants which lack iron, yellow areas may appear between green veins in new leaves on manganese-deficient plants.

Copper (Cu)

Copper contributes to many natural processes including plant metabolism and reproduction. Copper deficiency is pretty uncommon, but, just so you know, plants lacking copper may have misshapen, yellow-spotted leaves.

Zinc (Zn)

Plants use zinc in conjunction with other elements to carry out more natural processes including forming chlorophyll. Zinc deficiencies look a lot like those of manganese and iron—young leaves turn yellow between leaf veins. Also, plant leaves may be smaller than normal with distorted edges.

Boron (B)

Plants don't need much of it, but boron does facilitate nutrient uptake and it helps plants to grow new tissue. With a boron deficiency, new growth crumbles easily and looks deformed; fortunately, it isn't likely that your plants will lack this micronutrient.

Molybdenum (Mo)

Plants need molybdenum to produce essential proteins. You'll first notice a molybdenum deficiency in older leaves; they will yellow and curl up around the edges. If the deficiency becomes severe, leaves will look very deformed before they die and drop off of your plants.

Nutrients for Plants in Soil

It's simple to make sure plants grown in soil get the nutrients they need. I prefer organic fertilizers such as bat and seabird guanos (Again, a fancy word for "poop"!) over synthetics for a few reasons. First of all, although synthetics often have much higher N-P-K ratios than do all-natural fertilizers, they often lack many of the essential micronutrients. Organic fertilizers, on the other hand, are naturally rich in micronutrients and beneficial bacteria because they are derived from plant and animal meals, marine products, and animal manures.

And there is also the fact that I am a pretty lazy gardener. See, because synthetic fertilizers dissolve so quickly with water, your plants just get a quick burst of nutrients and any leftovers leach away. With organics, nutrients are released more slowly over a much longer period so your plants have a chance to use the macro- and micronutrients as they need them. Also, when synthetic nutrients leach out of the soil, they leave salts behind. These salts can change the pH levels in your soil—and restrict your plants' ability to take in nutrients. I really don't like fussing with my pH levels much. And I certainly don't want to have to worry with extra applications of fertilizer to make up for nutrients that leach out of the soil before my plants can absorb them! That's where the organics come in. (But, if you do decide to go with a synthetic fertilizer, be sure to look for one with a high percentage of slow-release—or "water-insoluble"—nitrogen to cut down on nutrient leaching.)

Just as there are multi-purpose synthetic fertilizers on the market, there are also multi-purpose organics. One of my favorite all-purpose types is pelleted seabird guano. I throw a handful of pellets in with my potting soil for use with well-established seedlings, and sometimes I mix the guano pellets into water to make a special fertilizer "tea" for my plants when they look like they could use a treat.

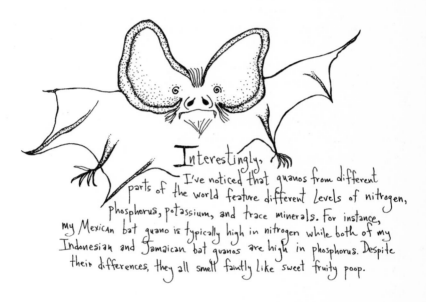

Interestingly, I've noticed that guanos from different parts of the world feature different levels of nitrogen, phosphorus, potassium, and trace minerals. For instance, my Mexican bat guano is typically high in nitrogen while both of my Indonesian and Jamaican bat guanos are high in phosphorus. Despite their differences, they all smell faintly like sweet fruity poop.

If you've used an all-purpose fertilizer and you notice a specific nutrient deficiency—or say you'd like to give your flowers a boost of phosphorus for a little extra oomph—you can supplement certain essentials organically, too. For example, in addition to some bat guanos, bone meal is high in phosphorus. For extra nitrogen you can offer your plants nitrogen-rich blood meal. Even simple Epsom salts can be very helpful; the mineral is rich in sulfur and magnesium.

Nutrients in Hydroponics

There isn't much guesswork involved with hydroponic nutrients. Gardeners using hydroponics systems have access to a wide range of fertilizer solutions depending on the types of plants they are growing as well as their plants' particular stage in life. For instance, very young plants require a much weaker nutrient solution than do older plants. And nutrient formulas designed to stimulate fruiting and flowering will have a higher phosphorus content than, say, those made for plants in the vegetative growth stage.

Whether liquid or granular, hydroponic nutrients often come in two or more separate parts to be mixed a little at a time as needed. That's because if they are stored in the same container for long periods, some macro- and micronutrients will chemically bind to one another rendering them useless to your plants.

Hydroponic nutrients can be organic or synthetic, but, in hydroponics, high quality synthetic nutrients are often easier to work with since, unlike many organic types, synthetics are less likely to clog the delicate mister nozzles and pipes in some hydroponics systems. Still, not just any synthetic fertilizer will do. Those that are low in quality can leave residues that won't dissolve—causing yucky build-up that will require more frequent cleaning of your system. (I'd rather spend more time gardening and less time cleaning!)

No matter if you go with organic or synthetic hydroponic nutrients, read the labels carefully to see if you are getting "chelated" fertilizers. This is a fancy way to say that the hydroponic fertilizer in question has been chemically altered to make nutrients easier to absorb and more available to your plants.

To help your plants make the best use of the nutrients you offer them, make sure the nutrient solution is well aerated and not too hot or too cold. A good temperature range for most solutions is 60–65° F. Even though they will absorb the nutrients at different rates according to what they need, you can avoid imbalances by offering your plants fresh nutrient solution every week or so. When it's time to get rid of used nutrient solution, you can apply it to your outside garden without causing any problems, but it's never a good idea to pour it on your houseplants or down the drain into a septic system.

Metric Mayhem

I don't know about you, but when I was a kid in public school, my classmates and I were at the mercy of the metric system. Although our teachers seemed just as confused as we were, they put on brave faces and cajoled us to convert inches to centimeters, yards to meters, gallons to liters, and back again. Even now I wonder: who had come up with these cruel exercises and why? I suspect it was a state or federal mandate or, more likely, my teachers were receiving bribes from some standardized measurements cabal.

Then, nearly as swiftly as the punishment had been introduced, it was stopped without fanfare or explanation. I was greatly relieved, and now, for better or worse, I cling to gallons, pounds, cups, teaspoons, and inches with the tenacity of a tick.

Interestingly, in 1902, Congress almost passed a law requiring the U.S. government to use the metric system exclusively, but it was defeated by a single vote. Poor little metric system...

Meanwhile, the rest of the civilized world has wholly embraced the metric system because it is purportedly simpler to use than the old English standards of measurement. You can imagine my dismay when I realized that many of my nutrients—especially those meant for use in hydroponics systems—required me to be relatively comfortable with liters, milliliters, cubic meters—in short, the metric system all over again!

Still, I wasn't about to let that stand in my way, and neither should you. If your liquid nutrients come in liters instead of gallons, your mixing instructions will likely require you to add a certain number of milliliters per every liter of water. This is actually no trouble at all if you can find and use a metric-standard liquid measuring set.

But, if you can't find one or you flatly refuse to use the metric system, you may have to convert from liters to gallons, milliliters to teaspoons, and so on.

Check out the appendix for U.S.-to-metric and metric-to-U.S. tables. Good carpenters measure twice and cut once. Likewise, if you are converting from metrics to U.S. standards, you are wise to do the math twice and mix only once. (Believe me, your plants will notice if you made a mistake!)

The pHacts on pH

Aside from providing the right kinds and amounts of nutrients, the right pH level is critical, too. If the pH of your soil or nutrient solution is too high or too low, your plants won't be able to take in nutrients as well as they should.

The pH scale looks something like this

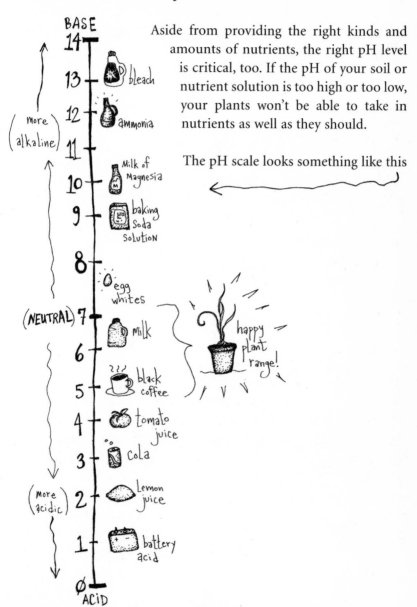

BASE

14

13 — bleach

12 — ammonia

(more)
(alkaline)

11

10 — Milk of Magnesia

9 — baking Soda Solution

8

egg whites

(NEUTRAL) 7 — milk

6

5 — black coffee

4 — tomato juice

3 — cola

(more)
(acidic) 2 — Lemon juice

1 — battery acid

Ø

ACID

happy plant range!

On the pH scale, 0 represents the most acidic and 14 represents the most basic or alkaline extremes. A pH of 7 is considered neutral. The distance between every whole number on the scale represents a tenfold change in acidity or alkalinity. For instance, soil that is pH 4 is ten times more acid than soil with a pH of 5, and soil that is pH 3 is 100 times more acid than the pH 5 soil. Most plants grow best within a pH range between pH 5 and pH 7.

If your pH drops below pH 5, aluminum and manganese can become available to your plants at toxic levels while phosphorus is rendered completely unavailable. Also, the availability of essentials including nitrogen, sulfur, calcium, magnesium, potassium, and molybdenum will be greatly restricted below pH 5. Finally, in lower pH conditions, beneficial bacteria will not thrive, but harmful fungi will. And if your pH climbs above 7? Manganese, zinc, iron, copper, and boron are much less available to your plants.

pH in Soil

Most commercially available potting soils already have a pH near neutral. Because supplemental nutrients and indoor growing conditions can affect pH, it's a good idea to test your soil about every other week. One way to do this is with a pH test kit. There are many different kinds of pH test kits available, and, for the most part, they all operate the same way—that is, with your moistened soil sample, litmus paper test strips, and a pH color chart. Your soil sample will react with chemicals in the test strip to cause it to change color, and then you compare the color of your test strip against the provided color chart. Most of the pH test kit color charts I've used represent acids with pink hues, neutral pH with yellow shades, and alkaline pH levels with pale blue colors, but this isn't a hard-and-fast standard. You will get a fairly precise assessment of your soil pH with this type of test kit.

Because they don't have to do any mixing or squinting at color charts, many indoor gardeners prefer mechanical or electronic pH meters. To use one of these you simply insert the pH meter's probes directly into the soil and wait a few seconds for the reading to show up. Don't worry too much if you discover that your pH is too high or too low. It can be adjusted fairly easily.

If you find that your soil is too acidic or too alkaline, you can make incremental changes in a few ways. For indoor gardeners with lots of plants, pH levels can be raised naturally with dolomite lime or lowered with peat moss or sulfur. If you have a smaller number of plants or want extra precision, you might try a pH stabilizing solution designed for use in soil.

Finally, you can help maintain stable pH levels by physically eliminating some of the build-up of nutrient-derived salts in the soil. You'll typically notice the evidence of this build-up around the edges of clay pots, and you can replace the harmful salts by removing about an inch of soil from each of your potted plants and adding fresh worm castings in its place to replenish lost nutrients.

pH in Hydroponics

In hydroponics systems, the rate at which your plants absorb different nutrients, nutrient temperature, and evaporation all affect pH levels. Because pH levels can fluctuate much more rapidly, hydroponic gardeners need to test them every couple of days. This makes using litmus paper pH tests pretty impractical. Instead, most use handheld monitors or pH monitors that remain directly in the nutrient bath to offer continuous readings. If you find that your solution is too acidic or too alkaline, you can make incremental changes in pH with pH up or pH down solutions. Many pH up solutions contain potassium bicarbonate, and pH down products usually contain citric acid. By following the label directions, you can raise or lower your pH very precisely.

You can prevent some pH drift even before you mix your nutrient solution by taking a pH reading of the water you'll be using and adjusting it as needed. Also, never use hot water when mixing hydroponics nutrient because the scaly stuff you see on the inside of hot water pipes is a form of calcium that will raise your pH way too much.

Planning on using rockwool? Because it's inherently alkaline, it, too, can cause pH shifts. To reduce them be sure to pre-soak your rockwool for 24 hours, and use a nutrient which is specifically formulated for rockwool.

One More Thing...

Unlike a fine Cabernet Sauvignon, most nutrients—especially nutrients for use in hydroponics—do not improve with age. The shelf life of your nutrients will depend on their type and treatment. In general, heat, light, and moisture can weaken dry and liquid, organic and chemical nutrients.

Tempted to open your nutrients before you are ready to use them? Don't. That can introduce bacteria or other unwanted substances into the mix so it's really best to leave them sealed until feeding time. To preserve their strength, keep liquid nutrients sealed and store opened bags or boxes of dry nutrients in airtight containers inside a dark closet or cabinet when you aren't using them.

Over time liquid nutrients can crystallize—costing some potency. Shaking liquid fertilizers well before each use can help re-emulsify stratified nutrients. Some liquid products benefit from refrigeration; once opened, some rooting gels can be preserved this way for up to a year. And as to liquid organic versus chemical nutrients? Organics don't always last as long; in warm conditions, bottled organics can bloat or bloom. Gross! But you have been warned.

Finally, even if you think you have stored them properly, be careful when using old nutrients. It won't hurt to test them on one or two plants before taking a chance on the entire garden.

There is a little debate going on amongst some gardeners with too much time on their hands. Here it is: Which lasts longer, dry or liquid nutrients? Well, both forms of nutrients do degrade with time, but the relative temperature and humidity of your storage conditions will impact each to a different extent. For instance, dry nutrients tolerate extreme temperatures better than liquid nutrients can, but high humidity will shorten the shelf life of granulate nutrients. So is one kind better than another? Your guess is as good as mine!

Playing God: Environmental Controls

Chapter 6

You gain a new respect for the order of the universe when you try to run a little portion of it all by yourself.

In your indoor garden you have to control everything for your plants—right down to the air they breathe. The funny part is, just when you think you have all the details covered—lighting, nutrients, pH levels, and the rest—things invariably change. And those changes will have little to do with your indoor gardening techniques. Rather, they are the inevitable result of your success. As your plants keep growing and g r o w i n g and g r o w i n g, they actually change the environment around them. The remedial science student in me chalks it all up to plant breath.

Here's what I mean. Plants "breathe" or transpire by way of tiny pores on the undersides of their leaves. So, carbon dioxide is able to pass into the plant through each pore, and oxygen and water from within the plant are able to escape into the air. In turn, water is pulled up through plant roots to replace the water that has passed through the plant's pores or "stomata".

This process is called transpiration and is responsible for keeping the plant cool, maintaining plant structure, and distributing minerals from the soil as well as sugars and plant chemicals throughout the plant. In other words? As they grow, your plants are sucking up all the carbon dioxide they can, and, meanwhile, they're releasing oxygen and water vapor—causing the carbon dioxide levels immediately around them to fall and the humidity in the grow room to rise.

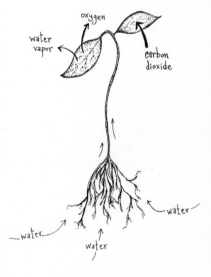

Still not sure what all the fuss is about? Plants use the carbon dioxide nearest to them and once it's used up, it's used up. They can't very well walk over to a different part of the grow room to find some more. Without enough carbon dioxide around them, your plants' rate of transpiration — and growth! — slows way down.

Temperature & Humidity

Lack of proper ventilation and air circulation will slow transpiration in other ways, too. You've probably heard your Aunt Esther complain, "It's not the heat so much as it is the humidity!" Well, for your plants, both mean trouble.

"It's Not the HEAT so much as it is the HUMIDITY"

A plant's transpiration rate is affected by temperature and humidity because both affect the extent to which water evaporates. Dry, hot conditions cause plants to transpire more quickly than do moist, cool conditions.

In other words, lower humidity causes more water and nutrients to be drawn through plant roots, and higher humidity slows this process.

Here's a good guideline to follow: if the surroundings feel too hot or muggy for you, conditions are probably unpleasant for your plants as well. Most plants grow best in an environment with a temperature range between 65° F during the lights-off phase to 82° F when lights are running. Temperatures falling below 60° F or rising above 90° F will adversely affect the relative humidity in the grow room.

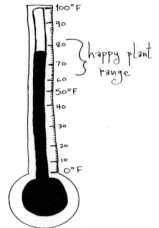

Relative what? To understand relative humidity, just remember that hot air can hold a lot more moisture than cold air can. So let's say the air in your grow room is very warm. Water will evaporate from your plants fairly quickly. What would happen if the temperature were to drop a great deal? The air can't hold as much moisture, and all that water has to go somewhere, right? The moisture condenses out of the air—dampening the walls, your equipment, and your plants.

Relative humidity is always a measure of this relationship:

$$\frac{\text{how much moisture is actually in the air}}{\text{the maximum possible amount of moisture in the air at the same temperature}}$$

In general, plants flourish when the relative humidity is between 40 to 70 percent. Plants accustomed to warmer climates may tolerate humidity levels up to 75 percent, and young seedlings and root cuttings will thrive in humidity levels between 70 and 100 percent.

In addition to the climate in which you live, the type of growing medium you use may also affect your humidity levels. In particular, indoor gardeners using coconut fiber in their hydroponics systems are wise to add extra ventilation because the medium is so absorbent.

Besides affecting plant transpiration and growth, temperature and humidity levels that are consistently too high or too low can attract insects and can contribute to the growth of mold, mildew, and disease. Steady temperature and humidity levels promote steady, healthy growth because plants can transpire efficiently without losing too much moisture.

Taking Charge

Of course, for plants living outdoors, getting plenty of fresh air is never a problem because the wind naturally exchanges the air around them. But for plants growing inside? It's up to us to bring the fresh air to them with a combination of circulating fans and simple air exhaust systems. By regularly replacing moist, stale air with drier, fresher air, we stabilize temperature and humidity levels while helping our plants maintain a proper balance of usable carbon dioxide and oxygen. Keeping the air moving also helps stomata stay relatively dust-free so plants can breathe with ease. (By the way, it doesn't hurt to dust the leaves by hand from time to time just in case!)

If your garden room happens to be equipped with a ceiling fan, circulating the air shouldn't be a problem. No ceiling fan? One or two small oscillating fans will be enough to reunite the warm air which naturally rises to the ceiling with the cooler air that's left behind.

But simply mixing and moving the same air around and around isn't quite enough for your plants; you should also ventilate the area. From super-easy to more complex, there are a couple of ways to take care of this.

One indoor gardener I know leaves the door to his grow room open as a source of fresh air. Then he exhausts the stale air with a vent fan mounted in an open window like this:

Think you want something a bit more permanent? You can install a ventilation duct and in-line exhaust fan in one wall leading through to the outside. If you have a clothes dryer or a stove with an exhaust fan in your home, study how they have been vented to get a better idea. If you do put in a special ventilation duct for your indoor garden, it's smart to place it up high since that's where most of the stale, hot air ends up anyway. As the duct fan pulls stale air up and out, fresh air from the rest of the house takes its place.

What's more, it's easy to automate this type of system by hooking the in-line duct fan to a thermostat. Each of the greenhouses I've worked in has had this particular arrangement. Just as I would start to feel a bit woozy from all the heat and humidity that had built up, the louvered slats at each end of the greenhouse would open and an in-line exhaust fan on one end would kick on. All the warm, moist air was pulled out in no time—making conditions for me and the plants much more comfortable just like that.

With a thermostat-controlled vent, your indoor garden becomes somewhat self-regulating. If, for instance, you've decided you don't want temperatures to climb above 80° F, you can set your duct fan to come on as soon as temperatures exceed your acceptable range.

To keep the environment even cooler—and to prolong the life of your equipment—you can also choose a reflector and ballast with built-in ventilation features. Some of the fancier air-cooled reflectors and ballasts come with in-line fans and vent hoods, but if you already have a reflector and ballast that don't have any of these special features, don't worry. In many cases you can modify standard reflectors and ballasts with ventilation kits.

Aside from using simple thermostats, some indoor gardeners like to take things a step further by connecting humidistats to their vent fans or to dehumidifiers. Just as a thermostat regulates temperature, a humidistat regulates humidity. Want your plants to enjoy a constant 50 percent humidity? With a humidistat-controlled vent or dehumidifier, you can be sure the indoor garden doesn't become too dry or too moist.

Extra T.L.C? It's a Gas!

Chapter 7

If you are anything like me you talk to your plants. A lot. In my case, it's more a function of my tenuous grasp on reality than anything, but most other gardeners do it because they believe it spurs their plants to grow. One of the first people to publicly suggest that talking to plants is actually a good idea was Dr. Gustav Theodor Fechner, author of *Nanna: On the Soul Life of Plants*. The German psychologist thought that plants, like people, had feelings, and, as such, he said, we should talk to them regularly.

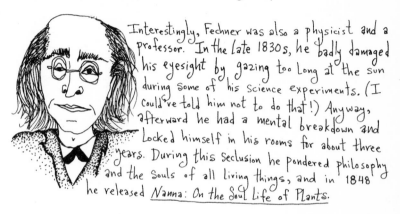

Interestingly, Fechner was also a physicist and a professor. In the late 1830s, he badly damaged his eyesight by gazing too long at the sun during some of his science experiments. (I could've told him not to do that!) Anyway, afterward he had a mental breakdown and locked himself in his rooms for about three years. During this seclusion he pondered philosophy and the souls of all living things, and in 1848 he released *Nanna: On the Soul Life of Plants*.

The jury's still out on whether or not plants actively appreciate lively (albeit one-sided) conversation. But, we do know that they benefit from the added levels of carbon dioxide that we exhale on and around them while we're talking to them. Of course, with as much carbon dioxide as they require, we might go hoarse or run out of things to say before we really do them much good! That's where supplemental carbon dioxide comes in.

Commercial growers have been adding carbon dioxide to the air in their greenhouses with great results since the 1960s. With elevated levels of carbon dioxide, the growers consistently noticed a boost in the overall yields and quality of crops such as lettuce and tomatoes. Also, flowering in roses, carnations, and other commercially grown flowers came on much more quickly, and the number and quality of their blooms increased.

By now, horticulturalists have had plenty of time to study the effects of supplemental CO_2 and the benefits are really something. For instance, CO_2-enriched growing conditions have been directly related to thicker, healthier leaves, more plant branching, and much faster growth. And, because insects seem to have a harder time wrapping their mouths around extra-sturdy stems and leaves, plants grown with supplemental carbon dioxide are also said to be more pest resistant.

Going Above & Beyond

Once you feel certain you've got conditions in the indoor garden just right (Light, water, nutrients, pH levels, air circulation, temperature, humidity—all of it!) and things have been humming along for a while, you can think about going above and beyond for your plants. Just as big commercial growers have for years, you can choose to offer your plants extra carbon dioxide if you like.

Not sure how much of the gas you'll need? Well, the air we breathe contains about .03 percent carbon dioxide—that works out to roughly 300 parts per million—and, although different plants may require carbon dioxide in different amounts, in general, most plants need at least 150 parts per million in order to keep growing. Even levels just over 200 parts per million can slow photosynthesis. When supplementing CO_2, indoor gardeners triple or even quadruple the usual amount so that their plants get between 900 to 1200 parts per million.

94

Parts per what? If you've ever bought one of those fancy water filtration systems and actually read the information that comes with it, then you've probably already heard of parts per million. Most often, scientists use parts per million to describe the concentration of pollutants such as mercury or lead in waterways. Parts per million (ppm) is the measure of the amount of one material within one million parts of another, different material. For example, one ppm is the equivalent of one cent in $10,000.

I can't say enough how important it is to make sure your plants have everything they need in the way of light intensity, nutrients, and the rest before you experiment with CO_2. If you don't? You'll be wasting the extra carbon dioxide—and your money.

That's because plants can't surpass their limitations. Let's say your plants are getting plenty of water, nutrients, and carbon dioxide, but not enough light. They can only produce as much food as the limited amount of light will allow, and increasing the amount of water, nutrients, or carbon dioxide you give them won't make any difference at all. If any of these factors is at a level below what the plant can use for maximum efficiency, it will only be able to function at that limited level and that's it. Capeesh?

Now there are several ways to supplement carbon dioxide levels in the grow room, and I'm only mentioning a few of them here. Some are really cheap and some aren't. Some are very precise and others…not nearly so. You can either produce your own carbon dioxide or buy it from a supplier as you need it.

Yeast-Beasties

Because CO_2 is a natural by-product of the process, fermenting yeast in the grow room is a very inexpensive, low-tech option to try. To start the yeast mixture, you just combine warm water, one packet of brewer's yeast, and a cup of sugar in a clean, gallon jug. Don't forget to leave the cap off completely or punch a small hole in its top to allow the gas to escape.

This technique produces an initial burst of CO_2, but you never really know just how much has been released. Also, a couple of times every day you must send in yeast-beastie reinforcements along with more sugar to keep them going. To do this, you pour out about half of the gallon and add more warm water and another cup of sugar. If you aren't sure if the first colony is still alive, you can also add another packet of yeast at this point. You can keep this process going indefinitely—if you can stand the smell, that is. As with your used hydroponic nutrients, you shouldn't put this yeast mixture into your septic tank because that could upset its natural balance of organisms.

Turn up the Heat

Running certain types of heaters in a greenhouse or grow room will also raise carbon dioxide levels. That's because carbon dioxide—along with some water vapor and, of course, heat—is a natural by-product of fossil fuel combustion.

By the way, not long ago, a researcher from MIT recommended that natural gas-burning electric companies start putting the heat exhaust they produce to better use by building greenhouses close to their power stations. It's really not a bad idea when you consider the extra heat could keep plants warm during the winter and offer lots of extra carbon dioxide at the same time!

Some indoor gardeners use heaters and stoves that burn butane, propane, or natural gas, and even small oil lamps can do the job.

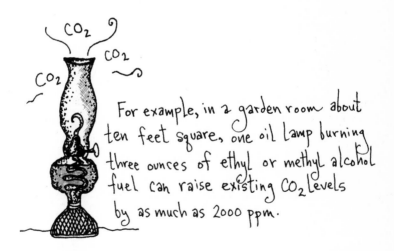

For example, in a garden room about ten feet square, one oil lamp burning three ounces of ethyl or methyl alcohol fuel can raise existing CO_2 levels by as much as 2000 ppm.

On a much larger scale, commercial growers frequently use carbon dioxide generators that have been specially engineered to maximize CO_2 production while minimizing the amount of heat produced. Smaller versions of these CO_2 generators are also available for use in indoor gardens that are 200 square feet or larger. But even if you do use one of the specially engineered CO_2 generators instead of a standard heater, you will still notice a rise in temperature along with your increased CO_2 levels.

Dry Ice

Really, dry ice is nothing more than frozen carbon dioxide, but it is so versatile! It's cold enough that dermatologists can use it to freeze-burn off warts and spooky-looking enough to be a must-have for theater productions of *Dracula*.

It can be purchased in large blocks and, as you might expect, it's also good for adding CO_2 and lowering the temperature in the indoor garden. To use it to release extra CO_2, you simply keep it in a sealed, foam cooler with holes punched in the top. As the dry ice "melts" or, more accurately, changes from its solid state directly to its gaseous state, your plants are exposed to the additional CO_2. But using dry ice to supplement CO_2 over a long period can be pretty impractical because it doesn't keep long and continually replenishing your supply gets expensive.

Bottled CO_2

If you want to know exactly how much CO_2 your plants are getting, a bottled carbon dioxide injection system is a great choice. They come with regulators, special valves, and flow meters that make them very precise, and they're well-suited for small indoor gardens since they don't produce any toxic gases, heat, or water vapor. Most indoor gardeners mount their CO_2 tanks on a wall and then connect the CO_2 release valve to tubing suspended just above the tops of their plants. (Because the gas naturally sinks, it falls right onto the tops of the plants.) Others release the gas without the tubing and use overhead fans to keep it evenly distributed.

If you go this route, you will have to get your tank refilled now and then, and that can be something of a pain. Also, this method is the most expensive.

What Now?

Think you've settled on a CO_2 method you want to try? Before you get too far along, you'd better seal up any large cracks around doors and windows in your indoor garden with caulking or heavy plastic. Otherwise, a lot of that gas will slip out!

Since your plants need light along with carbon dioxide for photosynthesis, it only makes sense that you'll be adding CO_2 during the lights-on phase and stop when the lights are off. If you are using fluorescent lighting only, don't bother trying to give the garden a boost with extra CO_2. Nothing too interesting will happen because most fluorescents don't provide enough light intensity for the plants to process the extra gas. Metal halide or high pressure sodium lamps, on the other hand, will.

The air temperature and humidity levels around your plants also affect your results with supplemental CO_2. Remember how plants growing in hotter, drier conditions transpire more quickly? Well, they do! So, if you keep your humidity levels low and shoot for 75 to 80° F while giving your garden its gaseous treat, your plants will "breathe" more rapidly and, as a result, grow at a phenomenal rate. And what if your humidity is too high and temperatures are too low? The extra CO_2 will just be wasted because your plants will transpire much more slowly than usual.

If you use yeast, dry ice, or bottled CO_2, you'll find that keeping temperature and humidity levels in check is pretty easy, but if you go with a heater or carbon dioxide generator, you'll probably notice the temperature in your indoor garden is trickier to control. To keep carbon dioxide, temperature, and humidity levels consistent, you'll have to coordinate your vent fans with the CO_2 system so that when the fans are on, the CO_2 is off and vice versa. (Otherwise, your CO_2 will blow out of the indoor garden before it can do any good!)

Now, if you've already wired a thermostat and/or a humidistat to your air exhaust fan, you can set the temperature around 75 degrees and the relative humidity at around 50 percent for good results. And, depending on the size of the indoor garden and the number of plants you have, you can expect to add more gas every two to four hours.

CO_2 Caveats

You've heard the old adage, "Be careful what you wish for because you just might get it!" It's definitely true when you're adding CO_2. If all the conditions are right, your plants will grow so much more quickly that they'll use available nutrients, water, and space much more quickly, too. You'll have to keep up! If you are growing your plants in soil, you'll have to transplant them more frequently so their root systems always have plenty of room to stretch out, and you can also count on having to water and fertilize more often. So don't go planning any long trips, OK?

Besides the extra work involved, you may get more than you bargained for if you generate your own CO_2 with a heater. If it isn't functioning properly, you may be exposing yourself and your plants to carbon monoxide—a deadly gas that you don't want around. Trust me.

I had carbon monoxide poisoning during much of my sophomore year in high school. The furnace in my parents' house was leaking the gas, and it simply needed to be cleaned—but it took us a while to figure that out. In the meantime, I looked and felt like a strung-out heroin addict. Mom told me to take off my bright red lipstick and dark eyeliner, but I wasn't wearing any. The wallpaper moved. It was nothing for me to sleep 14 hours at a stretch. You get the idea..

Always make sure your heater is clean and well-maintained. Not sure? Have it checked out by a professional heating technician before you put it through its paces, and, for extra peace of mind, use a carbon monoxide detector in the grow area.

Lastly, this may be hard to believe, but you can have too much of a good thing! Carbon dioxide can be toxic to your plants at levels above 2000 ppm and toxic to you and your pets at levels above 4000 ppm so keep it safe and sane.

Gadgets & Gizmos

Chapter 8

Some of the indoor gardeners I've met seem to like the gardening gadgets and gizmos more than the gardening itself. These are the same fancy-pants folks with closets jammed full of scuba gear, darkroom equipment, car stereo accessories, and the occasional yogurt maker.

I'm not really into having lots of "stuff" so I get by with just the bare essentials. I call these essentials the "Handy Tools" because they really will come in handy for you. And the rest? The rest I like to call "Fancy-Pants Stuff" for obvious reasons. The "Fancy-Pants" meters and monitors aren't essential to your success, but, admittedly, they are kind of cool.

Handy Tools

There are a few indoor gardening tools you probably shouldn't do without. Among them, a pH meter, nutrient strength tester, hygrometer, and a thermometer. And it is worth noting that some testers combine a few of these essentials in the same device. One of the more common combinations for soilless gardeners is nutrient temperature, nutrient strength, and pH. You often see thermometers and hygrometers combined, too. Very, very handy.

pH Meters

I've already mentioned a lot about pH levels in the "Food for Plants" section so if you skipped it, you'd better go back and take a peek! It doesn't really matter if you are growing with or without soil, you still have to pay attention to your pH levels. Some of your choices include cheap pH test kits or the pricier electronic meters.

The pH test kits are most often used by soil gardeners, but they will test pH levels in hydroponics systems as well. To use this method you apply your moistened soil or nutrient solution sample to a litmus paper test strip and watch as the strip changes color. You then compare the color of your test strip against a pH color chart to determine your pH. Although litmus paper test kits are less expensive than electronic meters, you'll find that buying kit after kit will eventually add up.

In the long-run, handheld pH meters are a good choice for soil and soilless gardeners because they are accurate and very easy to use. In either case you just stick the meter into the soil or nutrient solution

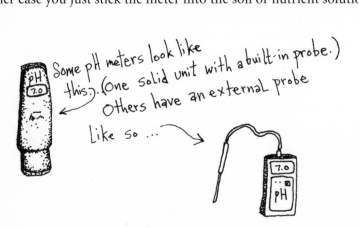

Some pH meters look like this). (One solid unit with a built-in probe.)
Others have an external probe like so ...

and wait for the reading to be displayed. Make sure the tester you choose corresponds with your growing method. Soil gardeners need soil pH testers and soilless gardeners need hydroponic nutrient pH testers. If you have a hydroponic nutrient pH tester, you need to store it in a special pH buffer solution to protect the delicate probes between uses. More expensive models are also made to remain directly in hydroponic nutrients and offer continuous readings.

Nutrient Strength Testers

Planning on growing in a hydroponics system? In that case, you'll definitely need to be able to test the strength of your nutrient solution because it is constantly changing.

(Hey, if you're strictly soil, you can skip ahead unless you're just curious!)

As the water in the solution evaporates, the nutrients become more concentrated. And, as the plants take in what they need, the nutrient concentration can, in turn, weaken. So how can you tell when things are out of whack? Well, hydroponic nutrients are mainly made up of salts, and salts in solution conduct electricity; so, you can measure the concentration of your nutrient solution by measuring how well it conducts electricity.

Hydroponic gardeners all over the world monitor their nutrient levels this way, but they have different preferences for the format of their test results. While most of the rest of the world uses electrical conductivity (EC), growers in the U.S. typically convert EC into the measure of the total dissolved solids in the solution. They represent this in parts-per-million (ppm). Whether they're represented as ppm or EC, these readings help us to know when it's time to add or change our plants' nutrients. In general, you're after a reading between 800 and 1200 parts per million.

You'll often find these testers listed as TDS/EC meters. That stands for total dissolved solids/electrical conductivity. TDS/EC meters look a lot like pH testers, and like pH meters, you can find relatively inexpensive hand-held models or go for one of the continuous-read, Cadillac varieties.

Hygrometers & Thermometers

Not sure if humidity levels in your garden room are within the optimum range? That's what hygrometers are for! Wine and cigar aficionados use them to keep their storage conditions just right, and you can use one in the grow room to keep tabs on your relative humidity.

You've probably noticed that your hair looks frizzier than usual on especially humid days. When the humidity is high, each of your hairs naturally contracts. Working along those lines, a mechanical hygrometer contains an element that reacts to changes in humidity by contracting or expanding; that contraction and expansion moves a needle gauge indicating the measure of relative humidity.

Wouldn't you know that the techies couldn't leave well enough alone? Now there are more complicated hygrometers that use semi-conductors to measure changes in electrical resistance. I guess they are a little more accurate than the old-fashioned kind, but they aren't cheap!

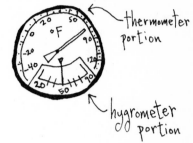

The inexpensive, mechanical kind of hygrometer often comes with a thermometer so you can check out the ambient tempera-ture and relative humidity at the same time.

And, speaking of thermometers, if you're growing in a hydro sys-tem, don't forget a thermometer for monitoring the temperature of your nutrient bath. Your roots can get too hot—and you aren't try-ing to boil them, after all. Plant roots prefer the 65–75° F because water holds oxygen best in this range.

Fancy-Pants Stuff

What follows are some of the items you can survive without—especially if you are partic-ularly chummy with an indoor gardener who already has two of each! As you become increasingly devoted to your indoor garden (and I bet you will!) you can think about adding one or more of these.

Light Meters

Truth be told, I think light meters belong somewhere between "Handy Tools" and "Fancy-Pants Stuff." They are nice to have, but you aren't likely to use one every day. Most indoor gardeners use them to make sure the light output of their lamps is still what it should be and to determine the amount of light plants are getting at different distances from the light source.

Nicer light meters have a separate part that you put under light and then a main part where the reading comes in like this:

There are also light meters that are all one piece. Some meters offer digital results and then there is the old-school variety which uses a needle to register your light readings. Some meters measure light in foot candles, some measure in lumens, and some will measure both.

Refractometers

A refractometer is the ultimate in fancy-pants technology. Because it can point to problems long before your plants exhibit any particular symptoms, a refractometer is kind of like a crystal ball!

Refractometers are so named because they bend or "refract" light through a prism in order to measure the density of certain liquids— in this case the liquid would be sap squeezed from the fruit or leaf of the plant you're testing.

To use a refractometer, you simply drop some of that sap onto the surface of the prism and then look through the eyepiece to see the percentage of the sample's total sugars.

eyepiece

test
surface

This number represents the amounts of fructose, sucrose, and carbohydrates your plant has produced. The higher the sugar levels in a plant's tissue, the stronger and healthier the plant. (A reading of 10 or below usually means something's a little off.)

Refractometers are great because they help indicate whether or not your plants are getting plenty of nutrients and how well they are using them. Because refractometers can be used every day, hydroponic gardeners really like them for measuring the effects of any fine-tuning they may have tried with their nutrient solutions.

CO$_2$ Monitors

If you're going to the trouble of supplementing carbon dioxide in your indoor garden, it would be nice to know exactly how much of the gas your green guys are getting, but accurate, infrared CO$_2$ monitors cost hundreds of dollars.

If you want a ballpark measurement of your CO$_2$ levels every now and then, you can use disposable CO$_2$ test kits. They're fairly dependable—give or take about 50 ppm. Usually they come with a syringe and one or two small tubes that are filled with special CO_2-reactive chemicals.

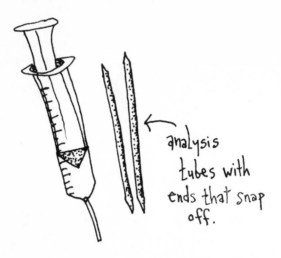

analysis tubes with ends that snap off.

You make sure the plunger on your syringe is pushed all the way down then you break off both tips of one analysis tube and stick one end into the tip of the syringe. When you pull back on the syringe plunger, you pull air from the indoor garden through the CO_2-reactive chemicals and, as with pH testing, a color change indicates the presence and the parts per million levels of CO_2.

Trouble in Paradise

Chapter 9

115

It's a fact. Bad things do happen to good gardeners. Even if you think you've done everything right, somehow you still lose all your pepper seedlings to damping-off disease. Or the nasturtiums have become so covered in aphids…those were the nasturtiums, weren't they? Not to worry. A few setbacks build character, and, besides, all you need are some good indoor gardening habits and a little diligence to save yourself from trouble the next time around.

An Ounce of Prevention

In part, your success will depend on what kinds of plants you choose to grow; you'll be better off if you pick disease- and insect-resistant strains. And if you take cuttings from friends' plants or if you bring something home from an outside nursery or greenhouse, you are wise to quarantine them for a couple of weeks so you can be certain they're healthy and bug-free—before you introduce them to the rest of the indoor garden.

Keeping the grow room as spotless as you can also makes a big difference. Never let dead leaves or other discarded plant debris stick around long, and don't you dare bring those filthy outdoor garden gloves inside! Ditto for the dirty, old garden tools. Clean them up with a non-chlorine bleach solution (one part bleach to ten parts water) first or get a separate set just for use inside. And, because they can bring problems from the outside environment to the inside, you should keep your pets out of the indoor garden—unless you have absolutely no willpower where Dr. Bonesly is concerned.

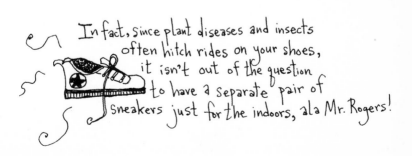

In fact, since plant diseases and insects often hitch rides on your shoes, it isn't out of the question to have a separate pair of sneakers just for the indoors, ala Mr. Rogers!

Now, add proper ventilation and air circulation, and you're almost there. What's left? Your rounds! To bugs, your indoor garden looks like a giant buffet so you'll need to check your plants for any signs of insect damage every day. If you don't keep close tabs on the growing environment, it might seem as if whole clouds of whiteflies and columns of aphids appeared out of nowhere, but, I assure you, they did not. You're to look for the usual suspects; I imagine you've already made their acquaintance in your garden outdoors . . .

Aphids

Aphids are easily number one on most indoor gardeners' "Most Wanted" lists. Their soft, pear-shaped bodies are usually bright green, but they can be bright pink, black, or gray. They're about an eighth of an inch long, and they'll drain the life right out of your plants. They look a little like this:

They lock their mouths onto the bottoms of new leaves and around stems and suck and suck and suck away leaving just a spot of shiny sap behind.

Spider Mites

You've seen teensy red dots on the undersides of some of your plants outdoors, haven't you? Those were probably adult, female spider mites. Not all spider mites are bright red; the eight-legged specks may range from pale green to brown. (When magnified, spider mites look like they are wearing backwards, hairy vests, but that's neither here nor there.)

If you have spider mites in the indoor garden, you'll notice your leaves will likely turn a mottled yellow or show clusters of tiny holes where the mites have been feeding. If they're left unchecked, they will cover your plants with their fine webs. Yuck!

Whiteflies

I hate to say this, but I think whiteflies are sort of delicately pretty. Only about an eighth of an inch long, the whitefly is soft-bodied, winged, and waxy white. They hide out underneath plant leaves, but if you jostle your plants a little they'll show themselves.

Like aphids, whiteflies also leave behind sticky residue. This can, in turn, attract certain kinds of mold. OK, so I guess whiteflies aren't that delicately pretty.

Thrips

Despite their diminutive size—each is only about one fiftieth of an inch—being eaten alive by thrips just sounds terrible to me. You really need a magnifying glass or, better yet, a microscope to get a proper look at a thrip. Six legs, slim wings. Here's one now:

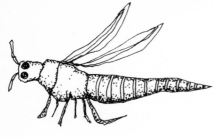

They have these sharp little mouths that they rake across tender shoots and new leaves, then they suck out the plants' sap. After they've feasted, the area dries out and the plant may exhibit white specks.

Closing the All-You-Can-Eat Buffet

All these free meals at your plants' expense need not continue. If you notice a few pest insects here and there while making your rounds, you can pretend you're the Queen and remove them with a damp towel—or you could just squish them between your fingers like I do. You can also trim off whole leaves or stems if you find a small cluster of bugs just settling in. (Discard this plant material outside, far from your indoor garden.)

They may not be pretty, but the same sticky, yellow strips people hang from the ceiling to collect flies also work on flying insect pests in the grow room.

If things get out of hand you can try a mild, all-natural insecticide, but use it sparingly. If you're running a hydroponics system, take care that you don't contaminate your nutrient bath with what is, essentially, a poison. Pyrethrin compounds are the active ingredients in many all-natural insecticidal sprays and soaps. They come from a certain kind of chrysanthemum plant, and they kill aphids, white-flies, and tons of other insect pests, as they like to say where I come from, "deader than a hammer." A series of weekly applications are in order so that you get the adults and their offspring in a few waves.

I am reluctant to spray anything on my plants too heavily because I am hyperaware of clogging leaf pores and suffocating my plants. The first time I ever used my own homemade insecticidal concoc-tion—you know, the standard dish soap/water/cayenne pepper thing—I transformed my beautiful sugar snap pea plants into a sea of dried, brown vines. (But, hey, I got rid of that bug problem. . .) Basically, I got the ratio of ingredients all messed up to begin with, and then I applied the stuff much too heavily. So don't go over-board, and do stay on top of your daily inspections—so you can avoid all this extra trouble in the first place!

Pythium

While you're checking for bugs, you're also looking for signs of dis-ease. Pythium is a giant pain because once it gets going, it's nearly impossible to eliminate. You may have heard of it referred to as "damping-off" disease.

It causes seedlings to wither and young roots and stems to rot. In older plants, pythium can cause root systems to turn brown, hollow, or eventually collapse entirely. If you've noticed your plants are hav-ing trouble growing or seem to wilt for no apparent reason, check the roots. Odds are good it's pythium.

Pythium spores occur naturally everywhere. They're in our water, our soil, the air, even dust. So even if you're careful to keep the indoor garden spotless, your plants are still going to be vulnerable. But it is preventable.

Soil gardeners, you must use clean pots and soil and provide excellent drainage. And for hydroponic gardeners? Keep an eye on the temperature and aeration of your nutrients. Plants that are stressed out from too much heat and not enough oxygen around their roots are easy targets for infection. Pythium thrives when root temperatures range between 68–86° F. If pythium hits a hydroponics system, I'm sorry to say, you just have to start over with new seedlings and carefully sanitized equipment.

If you have any infected plants growing in soil, first contain the problem by isolating them from the rest. If the infection hasn't progressed too far, you can apply a very mild fungicide and hope for the best. But any plants that don't respond to the treatment—along with the soil they were growing in—get tossed. (Again, far, far away from the indoor garden!) All that's left to do is sanitize their pots and any tools that may have been contaminated and curse the day pythium was invented.

Downy & Powdery Mildew

Both downy and powdery put the "Ew!" in "mildew." They look somewhat similar, and you don't want either of them around. Downy mildew forms grayish- or bluish-white downy patches on the undersides of plant leaves while powdery mildew dusts the leaves with circles of whitish-grey powder. If they're allowed to live long, both will substantially weaken your plants.

Downy mildew favors cool, very moist environments, and powdery mildew tends to prefer warmer, slightly drier conditions. But, even though they have different preferences about their growing environments, the good news is you can easily make conditions inhospitable to each of them.

For starters, don't let your plants grow too closely to one another. If you prune regularly—with clean tools!—you'll increase the amount of light and air circulation your plants get. (Light and air are mildew foes.) Also, keep all the surfaces in your indoor garden as clean as you can, and always wash your hands thoroughly before touching the indoor garden.

Think you've managed to get mildew anyway? If you catch it early enough, you can usually just remove the mildewed portions of your plants and sanitize your tools and the immediate area with a non-chlorine bleach solution. For more serious outbreaks, you can apply a copper-based fungicide for downy mildew and a sulfur-based fungicide for the powdery type. That should do it!

What now? You'll find some extra bits you may want for later in the appendix. In the meantime, it's time to get growing!

Appendix

So what's all this? From the straight poop on vermicomposting to those dreaded metric conversion tables, this stuff will come in handy...

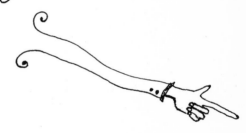

Vermicomposting

I mentioned worm castings or vermicompost in chapter three, *Down & Dirty: Soil Gardening Indoors.* If you garden indoors with a mixture of soil and worm castings as I do, you may find yourself going through bag after bag of worm castings fairly quickly. This expense can really add up, but you can generate your own vermicompost by keeping a worm pile or bin.

As if by magic, red worms (*Eisenia fetida*) turn fruit and vegetable scraps, coffee grounds, and other kitchen scraps into fresh worm castings and liquid vermicompost in a relatively short time. In fact, a single person's kitchen scraps can produce roughly four gallons of fresh worm castings in about six months. If you raise your own red worms indoors in special worm bins or outside in worm piles, you can expect to have fresh worm castings every three months or so.

For further reading, check out:

The Worm Book: The Complete Guide to Worms in Your Garden by Loren Nancarrow and Janet Hogan Taylor

Worms Eat My Garbage: How to Set Up & Maintain a Worm Composting System by Mary Appelhof

U.S. to Metric Conversions

	milliliter	liter
1 gallon	3785 mL	3.8 L
1 quart	946 mL	.95 L
1 pint	473 mL	.47 L
1 cup	236 mL	.24 L
1 ounce	30 mL	.03 L
1 tablespoon	15 mL	.015 L
1 teaspoon	5 mL	.005 L

Metric to U.S. Conversions

	gal	qt	pt	cup	oz	Tbsp	tsp
1 mL	.0003 gal	.001 qt	.002 pt	.004 cup	.034 oz	.07 Tbsp	0.2 tsp
1 L	.26 gal	1.06 qt	2.11 pt	4.23 cup	33.8 oz	68 Tbsp	203 tsp

The Endless Tablespoons

Even if your hydroponic nutrients come in standard English measurements, things can be confusing! The first time I set up a hydroponics system, I had a hard time figuring out how many teaspoons and tablespoons of different nutrient solutions I needed to add to my reservoir.

The directions said to add one tablespoon of one part of the nutrient mix per gallon of water. Since I had a 70-gallon reservoir, I decided to count out 70 tablespoons rather than bother with the math. (I lost count somewhere in the 50s after the phone rang.) Worse yet, the next part of my nutrient mix called for 2¼ tablespoons per gallon of water—well over 150 tablespoons! I ended up eyeballing it. Now I know there is an easier way. You can use this chart to get around all that counting!

	tsp	Tbsp	oz	cups	pt	qt
1 Tbsp	= 3 tsp	-	= 0.5 oz	-	-	-
1 oz	= 6 tsp	= 2 Tbsp	-	-	-	-
1 cup	= 48 tsp	= 16 Tbsp	= 8 oz	-	-	-
1 pint	= 96 tsp	= 32 Tbsp	= 16 oz	= 2 cups	-	-
1 quart	= 192 tsp	= 64 Tbsp	= 32 oz	= 4 cups	= 2 pt	-
1 gal	= 768 tsp	= 256 Tbsp	= 128 oz	= 16 cups	= 8 pt	= 4 qt

Let's say you have a 25-gallon reservoir and you need to add 2¾ tablespoons of a particular nutrient per gallon. That means you'd need 68.75 tablespoons in all. (I'd take the easy way out if I were you.) According to the table, 64 tablespoons equal 4 cups—which leaves you with just 4¾ tablespoons extra to count. You would add four cups + 4¾ tablespoons to your reservoir.

Suggested pH Levels for Assorted Fruits, Veggies, Herbs, and Tropicals Grown in Hydroponics Systems

(adapted from *Commercial Hydroponics* by John Mason, Simon & Schuster Australia)

Plant	Hydroponic pH
African Violets	6.0-7.0
Artichoke	6.5-7.5
Asparagus	6.0-6.8
Aster	6.0-6.5
Banana	5.5-6.5
Basil	5.5-6.5
Begonia	6.5
Blueberry	4.0-5.0
Beans	6.0
Broccoli	6.0-6.8
Bromeliads	5.0-7.5
Brussels Sprouts	6.5
Cabbage	6.5-7.0
Caladium	6.0-7.5
Canna	6.0
Carnation	6.0
Carrots	6.3
Cauliflower	6.5-7.0
Celery	6.5
Chives	6.0-6.5
Chrysanthemum	6.0-6.2
Cucumber	5.5
Dahlia	6.0-7.0
Dieffenbachia	5.0-6.0
Dracaena	5.0-6.0

Plant	Hydroponic pH
Eggplant	6.0
Endive	5.5
Fennel	6.4-6.8
Ferns	6.0
Ficus	5.5-6.0
Garlic	6.0
Gladiolus	5.5-6.5
Impatiens	5.5-6.5
Lavender	6.4-6.8
Leek	6.5-7.0
Lemon Balm	5.5-6.5
Lettuce	6.0-7.0
Marjoram	6.0
Mint	6.5-7.0
Okra	6.5
Palms	6.0-7.5
Parsley	5.5-6.0
Pea	6.0-7.0
Rosemary	5.5-6.0
Sage	5.5-6.5
Spinach	6.0-7.0
Strawberries	6.0
Thyme	5.5-7.0
Tomatoes	6.0-6.5
Zucchini	6.0

Nutrient Availability at Different pH Levels for Soilless Media

(reprinted with the permission of Dr. Lynette Morgan)

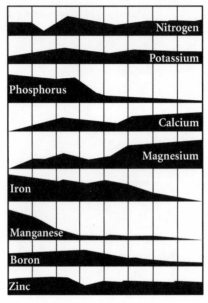

pH   4   4.5   5   5.5   6   6.5   7   7.5   8

This chart can help you to better understand what's happening with specific nutrients at different pH levels. For instance, with a pH level of 4—very acid on the pH scale—you see tons of available phosphorus, iron, and manganese, but very little calcium or magnesium. When pH levels range from 5 to 7, your plants get a little of everything they need.

Suggested pH Levels for Assorted Fruits & Veggies Grown in Soil

Plant	Soil pH
Asparagus	6.0-7.0
Bean	5.3-6.0
Blueberry	5.0-6.0
Broccoli	6.0-7.0
Cabbage	6.0-7.0
Cantaloupe	6.0-8.0
Carrot	5.3-6.0
Cauliflower	5.5-6.6
Celery	6.0-6.5
Corn	6.0-7.0
Cranberry	4.0-5.0
Cucumber	6.0-8.0
Kale	6.0-8.0
Lettuce	6.0-7.0
Onion	6.0-7.0
Parsnip	6.0-8.0
Pea	6.0-8.0
Potato	4.8-5.4
Raspberry	5.0-6.0
Spinach	6.5-7.0
Strawberry	5.0-6.0
Sugar Beet	6.0-8.0
Tomato	6.0-7.0
Turnip	6.0-8.0

Professional Organizations and Resources

Aquaponics Journal
P.O. Box 1848
Mariposa, CA 95338
www.aquaponics.com

Growing Edge Magazine
P.O. Box 1027
Corvallis, OR 97339
www.growingedge.com

Hydroponic Merchants Association
10210 Leatherleaf Court
Manassas, VA 20111-4245
www.hydromerchants.org

Hydroponic Society of America
P.O. Box 1183
El Cerrito, CA 94583
www.hsa.hydroponics.org

Practical Hydroponics
& Greenhouses Magazine
P.O. Box 225
Rarrabeen, NSW, 2102, Australia
www.hydroponics.com.au

Index

140

About the Author

Susan M. Brackney lives and gardens in Bloomington, Indiana. She has experience with traditional, organic, and hydroponic gardening as well as commercial farming, farmer's market sales, and greenhouse operation.

Brackney's other works include *The Lost Soul Companion: A Book of Comfort and Constructive Advice for Black Sheep, Square Pegs, Struggling Artists, and Other Free Spirits* and its sequel, *The Not-So-Lost Soul Companion: More Hope, Strength, and Strategies for Artists and Artists-at-Heart.* Visit www.lostsoulcompanion.com for more information.

143